Always Enough

Always Enough

God's Miraculous Provision among the Poorest Children on Earth

Rolland and Heidi Baker

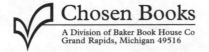

Chosen Books

A Division of Baker Book House Co
Grand Rapids, Michigan 49516

We dedicate our story to our many friends and staff who have worked so hard alongside us. They have selflessly come from all over the world to work for Jesus without pay and recognition, but they have been God's gift to us and the poor around us who cry out to Him. We owe them a great debt of love, and we know that their faith and labor have not been in vain.

We particularly dedicate this book to our two natural children, Elisha and Crystalyn, who have cheerfully persevered with us and often encouraged us to hold our course in faith in spite of all the hardships and frustrations. They are a joy to us and to Jesus.

Contents

Introduction

I (Rolland) always wanted to believe and live the Sermon on the Mount, but I was usually told that it did not mean all that I thought it meant and that I needed to be practical. I would read the Scriptures longingly, trying to imagine how wonderful it would be not to worry about anything, safe and secure in the presence of Jesus all the time. Miracles would be normal. Love would be natural. We could always give and never lose. We could be lied to, cheated and stolen from, and yet we would always come out ahead. We would never have to take advantage of anyone or have any motive but to bless other people. Rather than always making contingency plans in case Jesus didn't do anything, we could count on Him continually. We, our lives and all that we preach and provide would not be for sale, but would be given freely, just as we have received freely. Our hearts would be carefree in the love of our Father in heaven, who always knows what we need, and we could get on with the glorious business of seeking first His Kingdom and His righteousness. There would always be enough!

In time I realized that the worst possible fate would be to miss all of this. And so I began reading every book and drawing from every ministry I could that would help me live out the desire of my heart in God. Being raised in a Pentecostal missionary family gave me a huge head start. A tremendous formative

boost came from my grandfather, who told me endless stories
of revival, revelation and supernatural power encounters from
his many years among the poor in remote China. His book,
Visions Beyond the Veil, has influenced my whole life. While I
was growing up I became familiar with the missionary classics,
the biographies of early pioneers with great faith. I read the
sermons of Charles Spurgeon, *My Utmost for His Highest* by
Oswald Chambers and the miraculous story of God's provision
for George Muller's orphanage in England. David Wilkerson's
The Cross and the Switchblade showed me more of what was
possible. And I hungrily read modern accounts of revival, such
as Mel Tari's *Like a Mighty Wind.*

Giving up a scholarship and career in science, I got my B.A.
and M.A. in biblical studies at a Christian college, a valuable
foundation. But in God's mercy and grace I received as much
encouragement in faith from my friend and gym manager Bob
Zuver as I did from any academic course or book. Bob was a
prophet, struck down and blinded for three days when he was
called by the Holy Spirit through a Damascus road experience.
He hid away from public ministry and ran a gym and weight-
lifting equipment business until he withdrew to full-time
personal counseling. But his whole life was an example of faith
working through love. To Bob God was sovereign and strong,
His ways and wisdom past finding out without revelation. He
had no use for business as usual in the Church. By grace God
could be known, trusted and followed, and powerful miracles
could be a normal, daily occurrence. He used the strength
business to illustrate life in God. Regularly, almost daily, I
witnessed great physical and financial miracles in his life. God
also spent many years softening his heart and soothing his
spirit until, in all his strength, he became meek and gentle, able
to diffuse terrible attacks and injustice brought against him.
He is one more model of what is possible in God, a living
embodiment of the Sermon on the Mount.

I began to exercise faith, and my mistakes were mixed in with
beautiful victories. Faith involves knowing God well enough to
know what He wants, and that requires grace, revelation and

experience as well as knowledge of His Word. But I was excited and there was no going back. I was not concerned so much about what job I had as whether I had enough time to pray and seek Him. I had to live by faith. I could not disconnect from Him for anything. All I wanted was to love Him and feel His love. He could do with me what He pleased and send me anywhere.

Until I met Heidi, I had no close ministry partner with whom I could share a daring faith. I participated in the Jesus Movement of the 1970s in California and was deeply involved in large churches. But eventually I lost interest in big gatherings, huge concerts and constant socializing. I was willing to go to the smallest, most obscure meetings, if only the Holy Spirit would show up and touch me in increasingly powerful ways. I began to attend Dana Point Community Chapel, a church of two hundred near the beach in southern California. I was attracted by the glory of the Holy Spirit's work there.

On a church ski trip to the High Sierras, I happened to sit next to a short, very cute blonde girl and got to know her better. I had seen her often in our little church and was always impressed by her gift of prophecy. She was obviously intimate with Jesus, even as a teenager, and I could see she had a fiery determination to serve God. Every weekend and vacation she was out on the streets preaching or taking teams on mission trips, and she trusted God for every detail of provision. Her testimonies in church were powerful. Now God put me right next to her, and we talked for hours to and from Mammoth. Later I visited her at her college, and then at her home in Laguna Beach.

I hardly thought of taking her out to dinner or a movie. In her presence I was completely caught up in the things of God, and that's all we talked about. I joined her on an Easter mission trip to a poor community of local Hawaiians on the north shore of Oahu and saw her gift of leadership. Mostly I was moved by her childlike love for God, a pure, emotional force that overruled all other passions in her life. She could sing, and she worshiped with her voice at every opportunity. When I approached her house to see her again, I could hear songs of love float out of the window to her bedroom, where she would be on her knees with hands raised before her Jesus by the hour.

She knew God's voice, and He most often spoke to her as she worshiped. She was connected to Him in a rare and beautiful way. I began to love this girl whose heart so valued all the things that were important to me as well. I knew I could minister together with her, and I could travel with her and depend on the Lord with her for everything. But I was twelve years older than she was. And I was even a friend of her ex-fiancé, whom she had broken up with at the Lord's direction because he didn't have the same call on his life. But, amazingly to me, Jesus was bringing Heidi and me closer and closer together, until I realized that God intended us to be together for life and serve Him with one heart and spirit. I didn't know until I asked Heidi to marry me that He had already told her what would happen. In fact, He had spoken to her with an audible voice while she was on a mission trip to Mexico City when she still wasn't sure of my last name!

Two weeks after we were married in 1980, Heidi and I left for Indonesia as missionaries with a one-way ticket and a few dollars in our pockets. Our honeymoon was a last-minute miracle of provision. Every detail of our preparation was equally miraculous. We were naive and had so much to learn, but we felt a very great joy in depending on our God alone, a feeling that we have never lost all these years. We have tried never to put pressure on anyone but God for our needs. We wanted to minister to the poor in the power of God and be able to bring His relief for their fears. Now, many years later, with much more responsibility, we still delight in putting our pressures on Him. We pray with all our hearts that our lives and work will not seem a burden to our friends and supporters, but that you will be thrilled and encouraged along with us by God's goodness. May we encourage each other in our faith until we all learn to trust our fabulous God in every way. We want Him to feel loved in everything we think, feel and do.

Jesus developed our faith over the years in many countries

and ministry situations for a reason. Today He has given us over five thousand churches to care for in one of the poorest areas of the world. We live in Mozambique, in the southeast corner of Africa, a land that has suffered horribly from decades of warfare and natural disaster. Finally the people are desperate for Jesus and no other. Revival is spreading. In large sections of central Mozambique and southern Malawi, we have simple mud-hut churches in virtually every village. They grow until there are as many as can hear the sound of a preacher's voice. More are being added continuously, and now others in countries around us are calling for ministry and help, desperate to be a part of this fire. The Gospel of Jesus Christ is enough for them all. He is good and faithful, the Master Lover. They just want Him. They have been poor and wretched, but now they possess all things in Him. We dare to approach them, we dare to preach to them, we dare to pick up the helpless, abandoned and dying, because He died for us and rose again on our behalf. We eat and drink from His body and blood, and as a result, there will always be enough.

Chapter 1
The Children No One Wanted

"Heidi!" I (Rolland) called. "You want a mission field? Listen to this! They're blowing up Red Cross trucks in Mozambique!" I was reading *Time* magazine's coverage of the civil war there, and I couldn't believe such evil. "Oh!" she called back. "Let's go there! They need help!"

That began our story in the world's poorest country, one that lost everything by trying to take what it wanted by force. We were in Hong Kong in the late 1980s, preaching to the poor and homeless in back alleys. We were going to London to study for our doctorate degrees in theology and plant another church among the homeless. But Mozambique stuck in our hearts. It was hopeless. It was bloody, broken and at the bottom of the heap.

We had been working in the big cities of Asia, places with huge economies and massive infrastructures. But we were restless. We knew there were poorer places, more impossible places, places with even less hope. "Jesus!" we prayed. "Send us as far as You want! Send us anywhere! But we want to go to the poorest of the poor, to the 'least of these.' We want to see your Gospel tested and proven where nothing else can work!"

And then for a few years no matter what else we did we kept our eye on Mozambique. We researched it and all of Africa. We studied statistics. We read history. Mozambique was in war, and we couldn't get into the country, but we got as close as we could. While studying in England, we flew to Tanzania for our first taste of Africa. But to us Mozambique was the ultimate goal—and the mission field of our dreams. Would we ever get there? What could we do there? Would there be enough of all that it took to be God's hands and feet extended to that country? Was Jesus enough?

Mozambique got its independence from Portugal in 1975 after wearing down the colonialists with guerrilla warfare. A severe Marxist regime was set up, patterned after and supported by Russia and China. But a resistance movement, the Renamo, developed and for almost two decades struggled for democracy against the communist government, the Frelimo. Mozambique's Portuguese-built infrastructure, unusually good for Africa, was nearly wiped out. Roads, bridges, villages, schools and hospitals were blown up. Savage torture and killing took place. Millions fled the country as refugees. Over a million land mines were planted, resulting in the world's highest percentage of maimed and disabled people. In some areas half the population died from untreated infections after being blown apart by explosions.

Two-thirds of Mozambicans are illiterate. Many teenagers have never learned to do anything but shoot an AK-47. Eighty-five percent of the people live in huts, and only five percent have electricity. Less than ten percent have piped water; the rest use wells, rivers and lakes. Two-thirds of Mozambican houses do not even have pit latrines. There is only one doctor for every forty thousand people. Most do not even have access to aspirin. Half the children are dead by age five. Thousands die of malaria every year. And without the protection of immunizations taken for granted in most of the world, they are ravaged by common childhood diseases as well.

The war shredded Mozambique's already unviable socialist economy, which after the Cold War was no longer propped up by Russian and Chinese aid. Years of drought added famine to war. In province after province across the large country, twice the size of California, children and adults wandered in blackened, burned-out villages, without clothes and food. Without international aid, half the country would have died.

By the early 1990s the people were exhausted. The warring parties were out of money. In 1992 a peace accord was signed, and in 1994 under UN supervision a new, democratic government was sworn in. One-third of the almost two million Mozambicans who fled the country because of war, banditry and drought returned.

Suddenly, in January of 1995, we had our chance. On short notice I was invited, through a mutual friend, by a South African evangelist to speak at a pastors' conference in Maputo, the capital of Mozambique. Within a few days I was driving with my friends across South Africa toward the border in a red Nissan pickup truck. I had waited years for this. What would Mozambique be like?

We had to cross the border before it closed at five o'clock so we could get to our first conference meeting that night, and we were barely going to make it. As we got close our truck faltered. The gas pedal was to the floor, and our tension mounted, but the engine only missed more and more. "God!" we cried out. "Get this thing moving! You know we have to preach tonight!" Now the truck was crawling and jerking as if water was in the fuel line. We coasted into the border station, and our poor engine died altogether. We were going nowhere. But the place was electric. Guards were racing toward the gate. Everyone was shouting. A helicopter settled overhead. "The car ahead of you was shot up by bandits! We're picking up the wounded!" an official yelled at us. Had our engine run, we would have been attacked just across the border, too. God protected us miraculously right from the beginning.

We pushed our truck around, and suddenly the engine ran perfectly. We had two minutes before the border closed. Should we go? No, we'll wait and drive in convoy, we decided. Mozambique's guerrilla fighters in the bush were desperately poor and survived by preying on lone foreign vehicles. The next morning we had plenty of company and no trouble, but the road to Maputo changed completely. Now we faced

monster potholes and bomb craters all the way. Burned-out
and overturned shells of buses and trucks littered the roadside.
This had been an intense war zone, and all was not yet peaceful,
as we had found out the evening before.

The landscape remained dry. In southern Mozambique rainfall is usually thirty inches a year, but there had been drought
for three years. Corn stalks were withering in the sandy fields.
Finally we got to Maputo, a beautiful little colonial resort town
before the war, lined with shady, wide streets and situated on a
bluff overlooking the ocean. But looking more closely, we saw
that Maputo was a shell of what it once was. Little had been
built or maintained in two decades. Buildings were run down
and gutted. Everywhere was the evidence of a failed economy
and a desperate, suffering people. A million refugees camped
in huts around the city, displaced by fierce fighting in their
home provinces and towns. Tens of thousands were orphans
or children ejected from their homes by parents unwilling or
unable to take care of them.

We started our conference in the biggest church in town, a
bare, hot, dark, cement-floored, tin-roofed structure about the
size of two high-school gyms in which nine thousand people
are often packed shoulder to shoulder without chairs. All
around in the streets children played in the dust and sand.
Refugees set up stalls along the roadsides to hawk whatever few
goods they could get together. The pastors came from all over
Mozambique, many too poor to have their own Bibles, but they
proudly wore their white shirts and best pairs of pants. These
are strong Christians, having withstood years of hardship and
persecution, and I wondered who should be teaching whom.
But they have been isolated from the outside world and have
received very little Bible instruction. They still have to contend
with the strong occult influence of traditional African religion,
and also a powerful and growing Islamic presence. I met a
pastor who was delivered from communist prison during the
war through an angelic visitation, and I was moved and
humbled by many such testimonies.

I was there to teach but also to investigate the possibility of getting land for a ministry base. We just wanted a foothold in the country, maybe a small building where we could bring in some street orphans and get started like my grandparents had in China. After just two days, I was approached by a South African electrical contractor doing business in Maputo. He was a "tent maker" in Mozambique, ministering to the local people. He came right out and asked, "Do you want an orphanage?" His church organization had just been offered one by the government, but they didn't have the resources to run it. Would I be interested? Of course!

Amazingly, I found a car to rent, and the next morning I gave it a real test. Maputo was full of potholes, but the road out of town to the children's center at Chihango was an obstacle course of deep mud, sand, water and crumbling tar through a fishing village along the ocean. I thought this center would be a minor example of emergency child care among many in a country with so many war orphans. I was soon surprised and deeply shaken to find out that Chihango was the government's best effort at taking care of its abandoned and orphaned children, and the largest such center in Mozambique.

My pastor friend and I drove in and around muddy ponds for miles until we arrived. There were power lines, but they sagged toward the ground barely hanging together. High tension components sparked ominously. Telephone poles stood barren, their lines stolen long ago for copper. We pulled into the compound and up to what might be an administrative center. Children sat around sullenly, staring at us. We found a couple of adults who briefed us on the situation.

Chihango was more like a detention center for delinquents: wild, abandoned, homeless kids, thieves and fighters from the streets whom no one wanted, not even the police. There were about eighty of them, living like animals. They defecated on bare floors and sat there warming tin cans over wood fires. There were no beds, no mattresses, no sheets, no pillows. Every night was spent on the cold cement. They were bloated and covered with sores. They yelled, kicked and fought. The government could bring a bit of food only three months out of the year. They still had to steal and beg.

The buildings were a shell of what the Portuguese had provided decades before. All was completely vandalized. Doors and windowsills were chopped up for firewood. Wiring was ripped out of the walls. Window glass was long gone. Roofs were full of holes. Toilets and septic tanks were stopped up and overflowing. Dead rats clogged the leaky water pipes. Well pumps and windmill machinery were rusted out. Light bulbs were gone.

Gangs and bandits roamed the area, shooting up the buildings at night. Witch doctors beat their drums and chanted in the villages all around. We found out later that demons came into the children's rooms to choke and terrorize them. No one could read or write. There was no love, no care, no hope.

And for these Mozambican children there were no prospects either. Russian and German groups had promised help ten years earlier, but they never returned. I had found "the least of these," the offscouring of the earth, children who mattered to no one, lives that were worth nothing to anyone as far as they knew.

I was told, even by leaders of existing churches in town, that paying any attention to these children would be a waste of time. "They're bad children! You'll never change them. They'll never influence anyone. You should work with nice children in the city who go to church and are in school. And you should spend most of your time with pastors and leaders who can change the country!"

I thought of where I had heard such words before. This was exactly the reasoning my grandfather had received from fellow missionaries and local pastors two generations ago in Kunming, China. He and my grandmother had arrived in a far corner of southwest China, determined to go to the ends of the earth to find lost sheep. But while my grandfather tried to start "real" mission work, my grandmother began to take in ragged beggar children she would find dying in gutters outside their small, Chinese-style compound in the city of Kunming. She would wash their sores, give them clean clothes and feed them. Two out of three died within days anyway. But soon my grandparents had an orphanage of about fifty children. They named it "Adullum" after the cave described in the Old Testament where David hid in safety from King Saul's threats.

The children were not particularly grateful or responsive at first, wanting mostly to play and just be children. They were required to attend chapel, but they comprehended little. Then one day the Holy Spirit fell on the children and overwhelmed them with conviction of sin. For once they lost all desire to go out and play. They fell on the floor and hid under furniture, wailing for their sins far into the night and then for days. They were caught up in visions in which they were dragged off to hell by cackling demons mocking them in their despair. They saw others they had known burning in the flames. And as they were about to be cast into the fiery pit themselves, angels rescued them and took them to heaven, explaining to them the glories of the Gospel of Jesus.

So started a spectacular time of revelation, beauty, power and love. The children were in visions for weeks and months, taking as little time as possible to eat and sleep. They knew nothing of the Bible, but from their visions they would describe in detail stories from the Old Testament, Jesus on the cross, the great tribulation, the final resurrection, the marriage supper of the Lamb, our mansions in heaven and many other scenes past, present and future.

For many years I had longed for a continuation of *Visions Beyond the Veil,* the title of the book my grandfather wrote about this outpouring. But I believed that if I was ever going to see such a wonderful thing, I would have to have God's values system. He loves to show His heart. He loves to take the things that are not and use them to nullify the things that are. He does not rest until He reaches the utterly lost and lonely. He overturns the worst that Satan can do and glorifies Himself.

I remembered all this the day I stood at Chihango, facing the most pitiful effort to help children I had ever seen. Were these the tools Jesus would use to turn around an entire country?

Were these hollow, numb hearts going to be containers of the Most High God? Would generals, presidents, government ministers and businessmen change their lives through the testimonies of these seemingly useless children, now so empty of training, character and virtue?

And how would Heidi and I provide for them? For fifteen years Heidi and I had lived by faith for just our small family. How would we repair and maintain a major institution and make it an example that would inspire a nation? Where would we get the love, the faith, the endurance to keep going? And there were thousands more children all over Mozambique who were just as desperate.

But I was excited. This was a wonderful test of the Gospel. I wanted something I could to preach to anyone, anywhere. I was convinced that Jesus was enough for this place and for all of Mozambique. And I decided to start at the bottom of society and work up, just as my grandfather had done. Chihango was perfect. I would take it.

But I would begin such an adventure only with my wife, Heidi, who with her faith and heart for the poor, God had been preparing for Mozambique all her life. Her story begins in the next chapter.

Chapter 2

The Call

I (Heidi) always wanted to know people on the inside. What were they really like underneath their style and finery, or their rags and wrinkles? How could I love them genuinely, without pretense? How could I get past all the teenage sham and social maneuvering I saw growing up in a privileged community on the beach in southern California?

I was drawn to the less popular, the less beautiful, those who were left out and ignored. I wanted to sit with the lonely and forgotten and hear their stories. I was restless, always interested in other cultures and languages, and especially the poor. I just couldn't sit around at home, absorbed in myself and my own world.

My parents often took me to Mexico on camping trips and had unusual sensitivity to the poor. Our family would stop off in Tijuana and other places, and we'd visit the dumps and shanty towns, giving out clothes. I was also shaped by my sixth-grade teacher, who had been a missionary to China. She had just come back from Asia and showed our class vivid pictures of slums in Hong Kong. I cried with desperation for the people who lived there, and even back then I told God I wanted to go and help them.

I always wanted God the whole time I was growing up. "Where are you, God?" I would ask, lying on my bed at night.

I prayed every prayer I was taught in my mother's Episcopal church. I prayed all the time. The Holy Spirit would touch me powerfully as I took the Eucharist. I was being prepared and called.

At thirteen I took off to be a foreign exchange student in Switzerland for a year. I learned German, skied, studied dance and had a wonderful time, but I didn't have to deal with deprivation. At sixteen I ended up on a Choctaw Indian reservation in Mississippi as an American Field Service student, ready to face another cultural adventure, only this time in an environment of poverty I had never seen in America before.

During spring break at my Choctaw boarding school, I was left almost alone and assigned the job of exterminating cockroaches in our dorms. Day after day I pumped insecticide and sprayed everywhere. Cockroaches were flying, dying and dropping all over me. It was terrible. One Saturday night another student suggested we go to a revival meeting on the reservation. I was ready. Anything to avoid more cockroaches. By then I really wondered what I was doing in Mississippi. I had always thought of myself as popular, but at this school I was the minority, I was resented and I was avoided. I was lonely and miserable.

It was storming that night, but I didn't care. I ran through the rain and puddles to the church and tried to sneak in unnoticed. But I was obvious, the only white girl, with sopping blonde hair. The preacher, wearing his bright, multicolored native coat, was Navajo. He was preaching about his days in the Indian power movement and about how much he hated whites. I began to feel very nervous. But then I took notice. He said he met a man who taught him how to see people from the inside, and how to love. That's what I had wanted all my life. He talked about our sin and our need for forgiveness and faith in Jesus. He gave an altar call. Nobody responded.

Then I felt as if a hand physically grabbed my shirt and pulled me forward. My heart broke and I burst into tears. Sobbing, I ran to the altar alone in front of five hundred Indians. The pastor's wife tried to calm me down and assure me everything was all right. "It's not all right!" I cried. "I'm a sinner!" It was March 13, 1976.

Glenda, the pianist, came running over and gave me a big hug. "I'm so glad you're saved, but now you need the Holy Ghost!" I remembered something about the Holy Ghost from Episcopal prayers, and I wanted everything. Glenda invited me to her Pentecostal Holiness church the next night. I was going to go to the movies, but not anymore. That next day I felt light and free, like a butterfly. The flowers and sky were so beautiful. My mood changed completely. I told everyone I found what had happened to me, and I wanted them to experience the same thing. I sang and sang to Jesus. I was so in love with Him. I couldn't wait for church that night.

Only about thirty people were there. It seemed like I was their first visitor in years. All eyes turned to me, the California girl in jeans and a short top. Obviously, I wasn't initiated. They invited me to the altar. Again a hand was pulling me. My heart was pounding hard. All thirty laid their hands on me and prayed for my baptism in the Holy Spirit. Immediately everything went black. I've never experienced anything so dark. And then in a few minutes all became bright white, even with my eyes closed, just brilliant, blazing light. I couldn't get out a word of English. All I could do was speak in tongues. "Now you need to be baptized in water!" they said. I just nodded, unable to communicate intelligibly. Out came water and a bathtub, and I was baptized right there.

I became a radical sponge for Jesus. I soaked up everything spiritual I could. I went to church every night of the week. I was ravenous for the Bible. I had dyslexia and couldn't read well, so the church got me the King James Bible on cassette tapes, and they became my most valuable possession. (I was later dramatically healed and could no longer see through my thick glasses. I became a straight-A student and champion speed reader at Southern California College.) I played them until they wore out. Pastor Roark and his wife took me under their wings and opened their home to me. They discipled me, taught me to fast and pray and explained the Scriptures to me. I became like a daughter to them, and I was thrilled. I could hardly believe something so wonderful had happened to me. It didn't matter to me at all that they had long lists of rules for what I could and could not wear. They told me I couldn't dance anymore, but all I could think of was how lovely Jesus was. I laid my dreams of being a dancer at His broken feet.

I continued in school, learning Choctaw and native crafts and leading friends in my dorm to Jesus. The thought of a life of ministry never occurred to me, because I had never seen a woman preacher. In May, toward the end of the semester, I went on a five-day fast to find out more from God about what to do with my life. On the night of the fifth day, I expectantly went to the Roarks' little Pentecostal church in the country and was drawn to the altar. I knelt down and lifted my arms to the Lord. Suddenly I felt taken to a new heavenly place. Pastor Roark was preaching, but I couldn't hear his loud, powerful voice at all. God's glory came to me again, wrapping me in a pure and brilliant white light. I was overwhelmed by who He is. I had never felt so loved, and I began to weep. This time He spoke to me audibly. "I am calling you to be a minister and a missionary," He said. "You are to go to Africa, Asia and England." Again my heart was pounding and racing. I thought I might die.

Then the Lord Jesus spoke to me and told me I would be married to Him. He kissed my hand, and it felt as if warm oil ran down my arm. I was overcome with love for Him. I knew at that moment that I would go anywhere anytime and say anything for Him. I was ruined for this world by His intense love and mercy in calling me to Himself. I was stunned by such a powerful answer to my cry. When His presence began to lift, I opened my eyes and noticed that only Glenda and Pastor Roark were left in the church. They told me I had been completely still on my knees with my hands lifted up for hours. I wasn't tired or sore in any way. I couldn't speak clearly, but I was laughing with incredible joy to think that God would call little me to serve Him as a minister and missionary.

God's word to me was so strong that I began preaching the

next day. I told everyone about my precious Jesus and His intense love for us. He had let me see His indescribable glory, and I have never looked back. I have given all I am for all He is. This is the great exchange. I do what I do for love. Nothing is too difficult or too simple for Him. He has drawn me into His huge heart.

I began talking about Jesus to everyone I could—on the reservation, in the dorm rooms, at my high school campus back in Laguna. I began to prophesy as I heard the Lord. I passed out tracts. And since no pastor asked me to preach in a church, I began preaching on the streets. My hunger for God kept growing, as it had done since I had first prayed to know Him.

I wanted to reach people for His Kingdom. I approached our Episcopal priest in Laguna to see if he would let me use a building so I could start a Christian coffeehouse. He was very gracious and accommodating and opened the parish hall for me. Every Friday night for several years I ministered to drug addicts, alcoholics, the homeless and the demon-possessed. I learned how to cast out demons and pray for the sick. The Holy Spirit was my teacher.

At the same time I started attending Southern California College, now Vanguard University. When I went to register, the first person I saw was Babe Evans, a Christian woman wearing pants, makeup and big hoop earrings. I was sure that I was in the wrong place! Babe opened up, "Hi, honey, when is your birthday?" I told her my birthday and she said, "No, I mean your spiritual birthday." The date was March 13, 1977— exactly one year from my date of conversion. Babe said, "Happy birthday, honey! Jesus told me it was your birthday today!"

Immediately God began to set me free from legalism. I learned that it was what was in the heart, the inner person, not outward appearances that mattered. God told me that He had led me to lay down all the externals so that I would long for Him alone. It was my heart that mattered to Him.

I began dating a guy and fell in love. We planned to get

married. However, six weeks before the wedding I began to feel nervous and anxious in my heart. I was in a deep, intense conflict. I had really wanted to take a team to Europe on a mission trip doing evangelistic dance and drama, but I had decided to get married instead. I adored this man with all my heart. I thought he was wonderful. He loved Jesus, he was gorgeous and he was committed to me and the call on my life. He said he was willing to go anywhere.

But as we got closer to the wedding, my anxiety increased. For the first time I felt the need for a prophetic word. But when I prayed all I heard was, yes, no, yes, no, yes, no. I cried to God, "I need to hear something!"

At that time I was in charge of student ministries at my college. My responsibilities included taking the speaker out for lunch after chapel, and during this intense period of anxiety, for the first time, it was a woman. Although I had been given the freedom to speak to the school body, we had never had a woman speaker before. I was looking forward to taking her out. I shared with her that I was getting married in six weeks but that I really wanted to go on a mission trip. She gave me an intense look that I still remember and said, "That is not God's character!"

I knew that was a word from the Lord. God wouldn't have me get married when my heart was burning to preach the Gospel in England and Europe. The Lord just took hold of my heart and said, "You will lay this man down on the altar for Me, for My glory, for My calling on your life."

It was like cutting my right arm off. I ran into the chapel and cried. I sobbed for over three hours, and I laid this man I loved before Jesus.

The Lord said, "Will you lay him down, and will you die to this desire?" I said, "Yes, I will follow You, and I will go where You go and I will do what You do. I don't understand, but I trust in You alone."

The Lord is always looking for obedience. He is always asking, "Who will lay down and die? Who will be obedient?" And He always has the most excellent reasons for His commands. My fiancé was not called to a life of foreign ministry to the poor, and Jesus was going to bring me someone who was.

After I broke off my engagement, I threw myself into every kind of ministry I could. At school breaks I would take teams on mission trips around the world. One such trip was to Mexico City. I shared a small room with two other girls. There were no sheets on the one bed in the bare room, only one ragged blanket. That tiny room was home to sixteen people. The room was so small that they had to sleep in shifts, and yet they gave it up for us while we ministered in the surrounding slums.

A day before we left for home, I went into a little Mexican church. I was lost in worshiping the Lord when suddenly He spoke to me very clearly about His plans for my life. Among other things, He told me I would go to Indonesia and preach with Mel Tari, a famous Indonesian evangelist who had been used to raise the dead. I had never met him.

He also told me I would finish college that year, one year sooner than usual. And then He told me I would marry Rolland Baker. I had only met Rolland once on a church ski trip! We had talked, but I had never thought anything more about it, partly because he is twelve years older than I am. What really shocked me was that God even specified Rolland's last name, so there was no ambiguity.

The next day I took my team to the airport. As we went through customs I was stopped because my visa was not in my passport. They would not let me on the plane. I had let some kids play with my passport, and the visa was missing. The rest of the team got on the plane, but I was stuck. When I returned to my hosts, I discovered six loving, romantic letters from Rolland Baker! Had I not been stranded, I would never have received them. I looked forward to seeing Rolland again and wrote back to him.

There was more to my connection with Rolland. When we met up over a Chinese lunch back in the States, I began talking with him about my teacher in sixth grade, who had planted a passion for missions in my heart even before I understood repentance and salvation. I shared with Rolland my desire to someday meet this woman again and thank her for planting that seed. I knew she had taken a risk by sharing her missions story in a secular school. She has been a great influence on my life. He wanted to know her name. "Marjorie Baker," I told him. "That's my mother!" he said. "She came back from China on furlough, and you were in her first class!"

Sometime after that, while I was worshiping in my office, the Lord spoke to me again very clearly and said, "Tonight Rolland is going to ask you to marry him." About ten o'clock that night, it was time to go back to the dorm because there was a curfew, and I quietly prayed, "Lord, I heard you and he hasn't asked me yet and I have to go back to the dorm." Then Rolland asked, "Would you like to spend the rest of your life with me?"

I was taking thirty credits that semester—double the normal load—because the Lord had told me to finish school that year. The workload was so heavy I only got to see Rolland once a week between 3:00 and 5:00 P.M. on Wednesdays. Occasionally we could get together on a Sunday.

My mother planned the whole wedding. I just showed up. We told everybody, "We don't want wedding gifts. We aren't registering for silverware or china. What we really need is our plane fare to Indonesia." We planned to leave for Indonesia two weeks after our wedding. We had no money. We had no support from any church. But we had a word from God.

Mel Tari turned out to be a close friend of Rolland's, and he was the best man at our wedding. He asked Rolland and me if we would come and preach at his crusade in Indonesia. Our friends were very generous, and we had almost enough money to go, but not quite. We were five hundred dollars short. One night we were having dinner with millionaire friends and talking about our plans. Suddenly they offered, "We would like to buy your stereo from you for five hundred dollars." Rolland had a great stereo. It was one of the few possessions we had of much value. The Lord spoke to me, "I want you to give it to them. You can't sell it." I was shocked. They could afford to buy as many stereos as they wanted. Besides, they had just offered us the exact amount we needed. I looked at Rolland and wrote him a little note. He nodded. We gave the stereo away and went home that night with a lot of joy because we didn't lose our chance to give. We needed the rest of our ticket money the next morning, but we knew there would be enough.

Right away Mel called Rolland. "Our photographer just canceled. You're preaching at the crusade, but since you're a photographer, too, would you consider doing our photography for us? There's five hundred dollars in the budget for the job." We purchased two one-way tickets and had thirty dollars left over for our trip. That was the summer of 1980, and we have always had enough ever since.

We've never tried to figure out how to raise support or get money out of people. We get great joy out of presenting the riches of the Gospel wherever we go at no charge. We are ambassadors and lovers of the King, offering the best for nothing. There is no better work! In return, Jesus moves beautifully through His Body to provide all that we need. He plants His own generosity in hearts around the world, and we don't ever have to worry whether there will be enough. We have been hungry. We have traveled not knowing where we would sleep from night to night. We went years without a car. At times we couldn't even buy a Coke or make a phone call. But we always had enough to do what God wanted.

For seven years we traveled around Asia, preaching and ministering through Christian dance and drama. We saw thousands come to know the Lord through our meetings. It was a fruitful ministry where we were free to use our creative gifts as expressions of worship, and we loved it. During that time our children, Elisha and Crystalyn, were born.

Then the Lord began to redirect us. We sensed that there was more to our calling. I knew there was more of God's heart that He wanted to place within me. Jesus told us, "Stop. You need to see the poor." Like the good Samaritan, we need to stop for just one. We need to look at each one. The Lord broke our hearts for the poor. We went to Indonesia and lived in a slum. I started a job program for Muslim women. They lived in houses made of cardboard boxes and little bits of tin and trash. The Lord spoke to my heart and said, "Don't bring food or money, and wear the same two dresses the whole time you are working there." I wore the same two dresses for over a year. My friends in the slums taught me their language. Every day I ate in their cardboard houses and drank their water. I got a lot of dysentery, but I won their hearts for Jesus by letting them teach me instead of trying to teach them. After I could speak fluently in Indonesian, the Lord said, "Now it's time to bring them the treasure." Almost all of the ladies in the community were healed and saved.

We then moved to Bali, a very dark and demonic place, and enjoyed an intense, fruitful ministry for a year until the government revoked our visas and gave us 48 hours to leave. We went to Hong Kong and had to start all over again with another language. That's when the Lord said, "Just keep doing what I showed you. Sit in the park and learn Cantonese from the people." The park was the favored spot for all the old Buddhist grannies to congregate. They didn't want to hear about Jesus, but they were willing and eager to teach me Cantonese. As I was learning from them, I gently began to share Jesus with them and pray for them when they were sick. The Lord started healing them right there in the park. The Lord gave me a great love for the old ladies, and they became my close friends. They were also the unreached people of Hong Kong who had never heard the name of Jesus.

So many grannies were healed that we started what we affectionately called our "granny church," and it began to grow. They brought me their Buddhist idols, and we smashed them to pieces in the park. We also ministered to drug addicts and the homeless. We gave them all food and love, and they taught us the language. We came as learners and servants, and the poor taught us about hospitality and generosity.

The Lord sent my wonderful friend Lesley Leighton to help Rolland and me pastor our church and work with me on the streets. Jesus poured compassion, sensitivity and revelation through her into our work, and together we nurtured a rich and warm family among the poor that we named in Chinese "the home of loving believers."

In Hong Kong Jackie Pullinger-To's ministry to the poor was a big influence on us. We always took our grannies to her church in the afternoon, and we worked very closely with her. Jackie preached, "You ought to live in the slums if you're going to work with the poor!" Rolland was away on a speaking tour, and I phoned him. "Rolland, can we please move to the slums?" He understood our call in the Lord and agreed. I found a filthy, black room added onto the top of an old building without an elevator in the most crowded urban area in the world. Even the most desperate of the poor around us didn't want this place. It was tiny, without paint, kitchen plumbing or electrical wiring. Its tin roof rattled in the wind. To go to school our children had to hike up and down nine flights in a dark stairwell filled with incense smoke and Buddhist idols. Our neighbors were prostitutes and gangsters. But our rooftop was home. We fixed it up and thought it was perfect.

We ministered in Hong Kong for four years until I got so ill I could not make it up the stairs. I was diagnosed with a severe immune disorder. My entire body ached. I could not see well enough to read, and light bothered my eyes. I had a fever for months at a time. My lymph glands were sore and swollen, and I was so dizzy I often fell over. I was not used to having others take care of me. I ended up staying with my spiritual mother and mentor, Juanita Vinson, in Fairbanks, Alaska. She was the first woman preacher I had ever met. Her life of miracles and endless love has always kept me inspired. She and some precious women in the church took care of me for over four months. I could no longer pastor my church, take care of my family or even read the Bible. I stayed in bed in a dark room and prayed and listened to Bible tapes. This time was very dear to my heart. I felt the Lord holding me in His arms and simply loving me because I'm me, not because of anything I had ever done or would do for Him.

Then in that dark room, in sixty-below-zero weather, God spoke to me about going to England to earn a Ph.D. and planting a church among the homeless. It seemed a strange time to hear about studying, since I was so sick that I could not read or even walk. God was teaching me more about trust. There is always enough of all that we need if we trust in Him alone.

Gradually I became well enough to return to Hong Kong and minister again. Rolland and I applied to King's College, University of London, to study for our doctorates in systematic theology. We wanted to learn all we could and be exposed to a broad range of thinking. We were both accepted.

In the fall of 1991, we moved to London. By day we wrestled with prominent theological minds. By night we reached out to the poorest lost sheep we could find, the homeless huddling in doorways, under bridges, in cardboard boxes and in tents along the Strand and the Thames waterfront. London got cold, drizzly and miserable in winter. Many on the streets had no blankets and only light, ragged jackets. They could hardly sleep. They would go months without bathing. Some just sat in their filth, their sores festering and their spirits degenerating.

Small bands from our growing fellowship would go out carrying bags of hot baked potatoes filled with cheese and wrapped in foil. But we didn't just hurry down the street tossing out food. We stayed and talked, making friends and praying. We would leave copies of the gospel of John and invite everyone to our home meetings for hot dinners and fellowship, worship and Bible teaching.

Their stories tore our hearts. One night while we were mingling with a large crowd, a young man named Steve took me aside and asked for prayer. He was so simple and quiet about it that I wasn't prepared for what he told me. His wife and children had recently been killed by an IRA bomb in Ireland. In shock, he had come to London, where his sister lived. And then his sister had been raped and beaten until her body was a broken wreck. She died after being paralyzed for a few months. But he prayed with me, and Jesus came to live in his heart. He determined to live his life for the Lord; he found a job, and his heart, mind and soul began to heal.

There was Harry, with his blood-stained knife, who had run away from an alcoholic rehab center but who found the joy of the Lord. Christina, a venomous, bitter lady on crutches, became a compassionate angel of mercy who would do anything to help people. Malcolm, a crippled alcoholic and diabetic, found his home in Jesus and among our London family. David, who had murdered his ex-wife's boyfriend and then joined the Foreign Legion so he could kill as many more people as possible, mellowed out under the power of the Holy Spirit. Peter had tried to kill himself four times, but Jesus let us rescue him from death and hell itself. Roland, Digger, Steve, Derrick, Mickey, Trevor, Henry, Joe, Evonne, Mary, Robert and so many others—these were not numbers or church-growth statistics. They were all down-and-out loners who needed the love of Jesus more than anything in the world, and we gave them a church in their midst where they could find Him, worship Him and receive from Him.

In our early street meetings in London, we ran the gauntlet of cursing, screaming, threats, stealing and violence. We were interrupted, jeered and ridiculed during every message. Criminals would pull knives on us in our own home and vow to break every window in our flat. The mentally ill would beat on our doors through the night. Our phone rang every few minutes with some new crisis. But we developed a church family that we came to treasure. The poor of London walked across the city, lame, weak and cold, to stay late soaking in the love of God at our home meetings and church venues. We celebrated birthdays, weddings, Christmas and Easter together. We sang, laughed and cried as one. We had city lawyers and university intellectuals sitting down to communion alongside the simple and the poor. We were a cross-section of the Body of Christ, and we were in love with our God.

In September of 1992 Rolland wrote:

We marvel when we exit the subway station out onto the street where we usually begin our outreaches. Not many months ago the people here were much like homeless street sleepers everywhere: silent, sour, broken. But now when we arrive a crowd is excitedly waiting for us. There are shouts of greetings as we hug our friends. The talk has not been the usual grumbling and cursing, but about what home meeting they are going to next, last week's sermon, new people they are bringing, what they can do to help. Believers' Center is their church, their family. They help us pass out flyers. They want to know how we are. They pray for us! And, of course, they eagerly gather around for the hot tea and food we bring. We distribute all the Bibles, gospels and tracts we have. We supply clothes, blankets and sleeping bags when we can to the critically needy.

One by one we get deeply involved in people's lives. We listen, we talk, we pray. Jesus brings hope and warmth, and then ideas and initiative. It is a special joy to have new Christians energetically help us with the counseling who only months ago were angry and full of self-pity themselves. Now they spark fire in the newcomers, who are moved by such evidence of genuine conversion.

Believers' Center is not full of well-adjusted, self-sufficient, "normal" folk who don't need much attention. We have to slow down and take time to lead each person step-by-step out of a usually horrendous past into an intimate, trusting, over-coming life with Jesus. It is a long process. The Lord has been so patient with us, and we have to learn from Him. At each service we see new fruit. Last Sunday an unusually strong spirit of praise and worship rose up to God like fragrant incense, reaching a crescendo on the chorus:

> "Shine, Jesus, shine, fill this land with the Father's glory;
> Blaze, Spirit, blaze, set our hearts on fire.
> Flow, river, flow, flood the nations with grace and mercy;
> Send forth your word, Lord, and let there be light." [1]

What a great sight to see all these once hardened, bitter sinners glow with God's life and love.

---

[1] Words and music by Graham Kendrick. Copyright © 1987 Make Way Music.

In January of 1993 we recorded a testimony representative of all that we were facing, and what Jesus was doing among us:

Kenny came over yesterday. He had just phoned to tell us his story, and we wanted to help him. Kenny is dying with AIDS. Sores have spread on his body. He takes heavy medication. Every infection is a threat. Discharged from the hospital last week after a long stay, he returned to his lonely flat to spend his last days. But five squatters had moved in, and under England's bizarre law they could not be evicted for 28 days! Kenny was left wandering on the street.

Last Saturday down by the Thames, he ran into a group from our church and began listening to conversations about Jesus. He saw patience and caring. Taking Heidi aside to ask questions, he was moved by answers he didn't expect. Church and religion to him had always been an empty sham. Growing up in a parochial school was a horror story of frequent sexual abuse and extreme discipline. Professional clergymen often chilled him with their plastic manners and inner coldness. Even the chaplain at his hospital vented filthy, four-letter language on him in disgust. He could not remember anyone ever telling him, "I love you." His family was hard. He had never even had a birthday cake. He responded warmly to Heidi, but later that night he reached his lowest point ever. As he shivered under a doorway, a passerby urinated on him as though he were less than trash. He planned to take his own life.

The next night he managed to bring himself to Believers' Center. People came up and showed genuine interest in him. He was impressed by the testimony of Billy White from New York, who had been saved from a terrible life of sin and drugs. But eventually he left without a breakthrough and was alone again. Just as he was about to swallow a bottle of pills to kill himself, into his mind came the distinct words, "Remember that your Redeemer lives!" Over and over again he heard the words, "Your Redeemer lives!" He did not know the Bible and could not remember ever hearing this phrase before. All night he was convicted as these words kept coming to him. He couldn't sleep at all. Finally, in the morning he found some privacy in a men's room and repented to God. A great peace came over him, which amazed him. Immediately he called us, and we explained that the Redeemer was Jesus, and that the Holy Spirit had touched him. Later, in our living room, we spent time explaining salvation to him in detail. He could not stop talking about this extraordinary new peace he felt. His sense of humor was restored. He was relaxed. His rage at government agencies, doctors, priests, squatters and others had evaporated. His concern for his flat and possessions disappeared. He hugged us and prayed with us like a little child. We gave him *Visions Beyond the Veil* and a Bible, put some things together for him and helped him get to Scotland to be restored to his family. We'll write him and pray for him, that the Holy Spirit will remain on him strongly until he sees Jesus face to face. Our Redeemer lives!

Rolland and I knew we were not in London to stay. We had a restlessness from the Lord, wanting to see the Gospel penetrate and transform even the most remote, hopeless situations in the world. With our King's College residency over, we commended our church into the hands of our copastor, Kurt Erickson. I loved our English family and wept my way onto the airplane when I left. My time in London was God's gift to me, and needed preparation for the fulfillment of His words that I would be a missionary to Africa as well. Mozambique, a distant, poor, almost forgotten country on the southeast coast of that continent, was to become the challenge of my life. That story comes next.

Chapter 3

Chihango

My (Heidi's) heart was burning up for these unwanted children Rolland had found in Mozambique, and I could hardly wait to get there. He returned from his short visit in January of 1995, and we began sending formal proposals to Mozambique's government for the operation of Chihango. I had finished my doctorate, and in August Rolland agreed that while he kept working on his, I should go on ahead of him. Yet again we were starting fresh in a new mission field. We had no plan, no money and no idea how we were going to get enough support to take care of so many extremely needy people. But we pushed ahead, counting on God to direct us as we went.

The day before I left for Africa I was given some money, just enough for an air ticket and a used four-wheel-drive truck I found at an auction in South Africa. With my friends Johann and Merilee, I drove to Mozambique, not knowing the language or the country at all. I had never seen our orphanage, but I knew God wanted us to serve broken and abandoned children. I had been praying for twenty years about going to Africa!

Another drought had just struck Mozambique. One-and-a-half million people were starving. The ground was cracked. Corn stalks were withered everywhere. Maputo was full of desperate bandits. Thieves tried to steal my truck three times during my first night there. One mission group had just had three trucks hijacked. A new friend of mine had given his brand-new truck away to missionaries working in a safer place up north.

I headed for Chihango right away. Bouncing over the roughest dirt road I had ever tackled, my heart pounded with anticipation. I got to the center, and it was in worse shape than I could have imagined. Goats were kept in some rooms, and the children's rooms didn't look much different. There was feces everywhere. The placed reeked. The malnourished children were fed one cup of cornmeal a day. They had bloated bellies and worms in their toes and feet. They sat nearly motionless, with blank stares. Would there ever be enough love, food, healing and life for such a miserable place?

I had half a bag of potato chips in my truck, which the children spotted immediately. I handed it over to them, and there was an instant riot. A pile of children grabbed frantically for the bag, and chips flew all over the place. I remember the kids combing the ground and eating fistfuls of dirt along with the few crumbled pieces they could find. My silent cry was, "Do something, God! Do something through me!"

We had no money or food for ourselves. We had no place to stay. I had completely run out of money when a lady I'd never met came running up to the Bible school where we had stopped and asked if I could do her a big favor and house-sit for her. As she left she asked me to please eat her food, as the rats would get it if I didn't eat it! She was gone for six weeks. A few days before she came back the Lord supplied enough for me to rent a flat in the city.

God began to provide day by day, so we were able to bless the orphans. I started outreaches in Maputo and took in more street children. By November we had 160 of them. Chihango became a church as well, and people came from all over Maputo to attend. We gave invitations to salvation, and after two all the children had responded. None seemed confused or came forward twice. I had never seen so much hunger for Jesus and for love. These children actually ran to church. They couldn't wait to get together again for more. They came to love me, my friends and our small staff. They raced out to greet us as we drove in every day to teach them. They laughed and sang worship songs all day long as they ran and played. No matter what happened anywhere else, I was filled with joy when I was on the property. It was really wonderful.

There still wasn't much at Chihango for the children. Their rooms were bare, picked clean by thieves. They slept on the cement floor with no sheets, pillows or even mats. There was absolutely nothing in their rooms. They had no clothes other than those on their backs. They had no possessions of any kind. Many of them needed medical attention. Some were missing limbs from land mine explosions.

I bought the children their first cups and plates. For years they had eaten out of troughs and drunk under faucets. We brought toothbrushes. We repaired a bakery that had been built years ago at Chihango and started baking seven hundred loaves a day, for us and for sale in town. We cleaned septic tanks, installed wiring and painted walls. We hauled beans and rice from South Africa in a used army trailer. We assumed total responsibility for the center's administration and funding. It had been treated as a correctional institution for problem street children, but we turned it into a Gospel center for desperate and unwanted children of any kind. We simply went out looking for the lost and dying.

Rachel, one of our early helpers from England, found Beatrice walking along the road, weak, grotesque and almost dead. She might have been ten or eleven at the time, but it was hard to tell. Her belly was big and bloated. Flies attracted to fluid crawled around her infected eyes. Open, running sores twisted her face. Her feet were full of worms. Lice and scabies covered her. No one wanted to get near her anymore.

She had been raped many times, and her mother was dead. Her father was an abusive, uncaring alcoholic. He lived in a hut, so consumed with his own misery that he was oblivious to the suffering of his only child.

Beatrice took refuge alone under trees. She was losing her

struggle for survival. When I saw her, my heart broke. I felt an overwhelming love for this wounded child. I saw Jesus in her eyes when I looked at her. I held her close and brought her home.

Rachel and I got lice and scabies, too, but that didn't matter. More important was holding Beatrice close and letting her know she was valued and loved. She so desperately needed to be touched, cherished and hugged. Our daughter, Crystalyn, just ten at the time, said, "Mom, Jesus wants Beatrice to have my best dress." She gave Beatrice her most delicate dress, flowered, with lovely puff sleeves. Beatrice treasured that dress and wore it until it was threadbare.

Beatrice responded to the Lord instantly with tears flowing down her deformed face. She was so delighted to know that Jesus loved her, that we loved her and that she wouldn't be raped anymore or live another night on the streets. Doctors said she probably wouldn't live, but she did. The Lord healed her, and in six weeks she was completely whole.

Another girl, Constancia, was abandoned on our bakery stairs. She might have been five or six. She was so traumatized that she couldn't speak. The Lord told me to chase her. I would, and she'd let me catch her. She wouldn't scream or cry out, but tears would silently flow down her sunken cheeks. I would hold her until she fell asleep. I understood the Lord's heart. He wanted to chase her with His love and hold her in His arms. She was filled with inexpressible grief, a most broken child.

Understanding this grief and what it was to be unwanted and unlovely, Beatrice reached out to Constancia with love and compassion. Even though Constancia couldn't speak, Beatrice would talk to her all the time, holding her hand and taking her on walks.

One day I was amazed to see Constancia standing in line to be baptized. I thought, "How am I going to baptize a girl who doesn't speak? How can she understand?" I asked her, "Do you really know what this means?" There was a line of over 120 people that day. I was standing in an old laundry tank. By this time the water was a murky green from all the people who had been immersed in it. I asked Constancia again, "Do you really know God is speaking to your heart? Do you really want to be baptized?" She nodded.

I simply picked up this frail, broken, beaten little girl and placed her in the water. In the name of the Father, Son and Holy Spirit, I baptized her. When she came up from the water, she smiled for the first time among us. Her face radiated the glory of God. That day she suddenly began speaking again and told me she wanted to lead the children's choir.

Later she also told us that she had seen her parents shot and their heads cut off. Until then we had no idea what horror had so frozen her spirit. But Jesus came to her in that baptismal water and turned her mourning into joy. Both Beatrice and Constancia want to be missionaries and lay their lives down for Him.

Other children continued to arrive, also carrying the scars of war and its continuing aftermath of violence and terrible poverty. In March of 1996, a very sad father brought his two-year-old son, Valentino, to us. The boy's mother had been beaten to death by three bandits while holding him in her arms. The destitute father could only turn to us. Valentino screamed whenever he was put down. Again our tears flowed and flowed, and we knew once more why we are in Africa. We are the physical extension of God's heart, rescuing precious human beings from Satan's incredible cruelty. I held Valentino whenever I could for months, and now he is one of our happiest children, almost unbearably photogenic.

We kept going to the streets to find more of these little ones, none forgotten by Jesus. I wrote in June of 1996:

Maputo is often seen as the promised land, where many "lost" children end up. We have been reaching out to these precious, abandoned children for many months. Our Chihango family is a place where there is hope for them. Trust is not won easily on the streets. Words are cheap. These children watch, wait and consider if they want to be part of our family. Today was a happy day. Six more young lives were born into the Kingdom!

Augusto, Joan, Adriano, Mario, Alberto and Guambe have become children of the living God. He will care for them and provide their bread, and fill the emptiness in their hearts. Perhaps slowly the pain of abandonment will fade as they are embraced by their new family, Chihango Arco-Íris!

Last week my daughter, Crystalyn, and I were out buying bread, and in the street we came upon a motionless boy dressed in rags and covered with sores. We thought this precious child was dead. I walked over to him and laid my hands on his shoulder. He woke up and looked frightened. I gave him some bread and began to ask him his story. Everista could not talk very well. He had not spoken for a long time. He did not know how old he was. He had never been to school. He knew his parents were dead, and he was alone and hungry. The other street children found him odd and had been kicking him around. His body bore the marks of years of abuse. His fingers were scarred from nervous chewing. He scurried along the ground more like an animal than a human being. I asked Everista if he wanted to come and live with us. I spoke of our large family at Chihango. His eyes brightened. I took him home and washed his wounds. Crystalyn happily gave him some clothes and things to play with. We hugged him and prayed for him and let him know he was loved.

In October I wrote:

Gray clouds blend into the grim streets of Maputo. Small children risk their lives running in front of moving cars, hoping to sell some cigarettes. Old widows sit close by, selling coal for a few pennies. It may take them all day to earn enough to buy some bread. Julia, thirteen; José, eight; Amelia, five; Moises, thirteen; and Boas, eleven, began today hungry, searching for food in the city streets and rubbish bins. These children are friends of mine; they often stop by the office and we talk and share bread together. Although these children have mothers, their fathers have abandoned them and they have never been to school. Tomorrow they will all come and live with us at

Chihango Arco-Íris. The joy on their faces as they think of being able to study and go to sleep with a blanket and a full stomach makes everything worth it. I am reminded of Isaiah 14:30: "The poorest of the poor will find pasture, and the needy will lie down in safety." The Lord has compassion on the poor and outcast, and He cares for them. As we have made friends with street children, our family has grown from eighty to over three hundred this year. While there is no special budget or great plan to expand Chihango, we do not turn anyone away. Our dorms are full, yet thousands more children roam the streets orphaned and abandoned. Please pray for the street children of Mozambique. We only need bigger hearts and more of God's people to care for all the treasures God sends us.

Chihango was filling up quickly, and by December of 1996 we thought we had reached our limits. "No more!" we insisted. "We're full; that's it!" We were bursting with well over three hundred children, many newly arrived from the streets and very difficult to watch over with our small staff.

But Chihango was known in the streets of Maputo. It seemed that wherever we drove, our vehicle was recognized and the children called out to us. One day five more made their way across the city to the gates of our little office flat, and there they waited patiently for us to show up and take them to Chihango. "Okay," we thought, "let's be strong. Let's at least interview them and hear their stories."

First was Tania, thirteen or fourteen as far as she knew. She didn't know where her father was, and her mother was dead. During Mozambique's civil war, she had seen many people killed with guns and knives. For three years she had survived on the streets through prostitution. How could we turn her away?

Then we talked to Annabelle, ten, who had never been to school. Her father had been killed in the war, and her mother had died of disease. On the streets for three years, for the past year she had also been prostituting herself to buy food. Since she was small, she had endured additional abuse. Both these girls had severe venereal disease. This is why we are here; we couldn't turn them away.

Edson was a thirteen-year-old boy who had only been to second grade. His mother had died falling off a train, and his father had run off to South Africa. He had been surviving on the streets by guarding cars for small tips. We couldn't help noticing sores on his back from infected burns.

We turned to Bryce, ten, with only a first-grade education. When his mother died, his father took another woman who didn't want Bryce in the house. And so his father beat him until he ran away.

Alfredo didn't even know his age. Someone told him he came from Vilanculos, a small town far to the north. He got separated from his parents during the war and didn't know if they were dead or alive. He had been alone on the streets for as long as he could remember.

And so we took them all.

Because of God's grace we saw Chihango renewed. It changed from a shell of an institution with a frightening reputation for starvation and cruelty into a thriving, hope-filled home for almost 350 happy and believing children rescued from horrendous backgrounds. They had faith. They prayed for their daily food. They knew how to worship. They went into the villages and streets of Maputo to preach with us. We had a clear vision for our children, once beaten, abused and starved: that God might "bestow on them a crown of beauty instead of ashes, the oil of gladness instead of mourning, and a garment of praise instead of a spirit of despair. They will be called oaks of righteousness, a planting of the LORD for the display of his splendor" (Isaiah 61:3).

Teams were arriving from around the world to help. Our staff began to grow. In the Spirit we fought off attacks of demonic power, waves of malaria and violent gangs. Our food supply stabilized after many crises through the intercession of our children and friends everywhere. We had made Chihango our home. We had plans for our breezy, sandy center by the sea. Our schedules were still impossibly intense, but we began to envision a more normal routine. In the southern hemisphere's winter of 1996 we wrote:

> Silvery mist lies low over the grass and rolling fields of Chihango in the golden dawn light. A brightening, rich blue sky is still the backdrop for diamonds dazzling in the heavens: a sharply etched new moon, the intense morning star and the elegant company of lesser lights. A warm assortment of colors from the rising sun splash themselves around the horizon on delicate clouds, artfully left by recent storms. Soft sounds of life begin arriving from the simple country huts of neighboring villages. Smoke spirals up from wood fires on dirt courtyards here and there as the challenge of preparing food for another day begins.
>
> The children are up early at Chihango. All the way from our house we can hear their shouts and see them scampering back and forth between the trees. I wonder how they slept, for the night was chilly and many are still without blankets, sleeping on thin mats. But the day has begun magnificently. We seem so far away from war, from conflict and disorder and all the evil legacy of Satan's work. May the peace of the Holy Spirit settle gently and sweetly on this land and these people.

We were Chihango Arco-Íris, using the Portuguese for "rainbow," speaking of God's promise of hope in Genesis. Early one morning during that time, I was driving our children to school along the beach. There had been a storm, and now the clouds were breaking up. The fresh breeze was clean and exhilarating. Everything was intensely beautiful—the rippling, blue ocean, the wet trees and green grass, the towering cloud formations lit up in orange and lavender. And over it all as a crowning touch was a brilliant double rainbow, touching all the way down on both sides. It seemed that all of Chihango and our work there was being cradled in God's faithfulness and glory. What an encouraging, spectacular moment. We revel in God's beauty, His goodness and the work of His hands.

But our lives were not to become routine at all, and, in fact, we were about to be radically resifted. We were working eighteen-hour days and often battling with corrupt government bureaucrats. We were quickly wearing out. I had served the Lord joyfully and eagerly for over twenty years. I had done everything I could to please Jesus in Mozambique. He was doing amazing things. But I was exhausted and getting steadily weaker and sicker. The constant responsibility of having over three hundred children looking to me as their "Mama Aida" had simply worn me out. I had been on antibiotics six times in two months for various infections and dysentery, and then I developed pneumonia. The doctors were concerned that I had tuberculosis. I knew I needed recharging and felt compelled to go to the Toronto Airport Christian Fellowship (TACF), a church in Canada that was experiencing an unusual, powerful, wonderful move of the Holy Spirit. It had become a spiritual "intensive care ward" for people all over the world who desperately needed a refreshing overhaul, and I wanted to be there.

I checked myself out of the hospital and got on a plane to Toronto. Physically I was taking a risk by rejecting my doctor's advice and going on such a long trip. My lungs were filled with fluid, and I could barely breathe. Financially we were very low. But I had to go!

Rolland had just returned from Toronto and had had a dramatically great time with God there. He was full of faith and compassion, which made me want to get there all the more. I stopped off in California briefly to see my parents and again was put in the hospital. I could hardly walk. It was very difficult to breathe, but all I could think of was how hungry I was for a touch from God. I was so sick and exhausted. I longed for a simple, nonstressful job. I had ten years of higher education, but at this point I didn't even want to teach, because I didn't know what to teach anymore.

When I arrived at TACF, I was healed in the first meeting. The Lord mercifully opened up my lungs and allowed me to breathe effortlessly for the first time in weeks. I spent many hours receiving prayer from loving people on the ministry team. It was deeply healing to be ministered to after preaching and teaching for so many years. Carol Arnott and Sharon Wright especially ministered to me in prayer for hours. I had never experienced such loving, compassionate, unhurried prayer ministry.

Often during my time at TACF, I was on the floor before the Lord, unable to move. His presence was so heavy upon me. One night at the end of a meeting, I was still unable to move. I was rather hidden behind the altar and began to get slightly nervous as Betty the security guard was calling, "Okay, everyone! It's time to go!" The Lord spoke to my heart and said, "I am sending a precious servant to rescue you." I couldn't even move my little finger. Betty came over and gently asked me how I was doing. She got a couple of people to help lift me into a chair. The love and mercy that flowed out of her was life-transforming. The Lord taught me so much during those times of utter weakness. His presence was so strong upon me that I felt as if a blanket of liquid love was laid upon me. He demonstrated that He is my only strength. He is my hope. I depend only on Him. I can do nothing without Him and nothing without the Body of Christ.

One night I was groaning in intercession for the children of Mozambique. There were thousands coming toward me, and I was crying, "No, Lord. There are too many!" Then I had a dramatic, clear vision of Jesus. I was with Him, and thousands and thousands of children surrounded us. I saw His shining face and His intense, burning eyes of love. I also saw His body. It was bruised and broken, and His side was pierced. He said, "Look into My eyes. You give them something to eat." Then He took a piece of His broken body and handed it to me. It became bread in my hands, and I began to give it to the children. It multiplied in my hands. Then again the Lord said, "Look into My eyes. You give them something to drink." He gave me a cup of blood and water, which flowed from His side. I knew it was a cup of bitterness and joy. I drank it and then began to give it to the children to drink. The cup did not go dry. By this point I was crying uncontrollably. I was completely undone by His fiery eyes of love. I realized what it had cost Him to provide such spiritual and physical food for us all. The Lord spoke to my heart and said, "There will always be enough, because I died."

I was refreshed and ready to go back to Mozambique. I expected to see a wave of new, amazing miracles right away. Instead, all hell broke loose! We were completely shocked when what we thought was a fairly solid relationship with the government broke down overnight. We were deep in the long process of negotiating a joint venture with Maputo's Department of Education that would allow us to develop Chihango into an all-around ministry center for Mozambique. Not only was our proposed contract rejected, but the government also issued us conditions for our continued work at Chihango. All religious activity at the center was to be suspended immediately. Our children were not allowed to pray, even under a tree. There was to be no Christian teaching, no gospel singing and no worship. We were told we could not employ older children who were out of school and had nowhere to go. We could no longer bring in street children, give out clothes or dispense medicine. We were given pages of restrictions, all aimed at removing spirituality from Chihango.

We were told that if we prayed, worshiped or sang, we would have to leave immediately. The children of Chihango reacted with intense prayer and worship, even singing and dancing in defiance of the orders. All the children united with us and said they would rather camp out with us in tents in the fields, with no water and electricity, than remain behind where they were beaten, starved and prevented from worshiping Jesus.

The community told me I needed to leave as quickly as possible with my family, because there was a twenty-dollar contract out on my life. After the war few were willing to give up their guns and ammunition, so AK-47s and grenades were common. Finding someone willing to kill me was easy, but I have always insisted that I'm worth more than twenty dollars!

Our Chihango family was given 48 hours to vacate. The children knew that anything they left behind would be stolen and sold. Our staff tried to save whatever they could—especially beds, mattresses, clothes, tools and medicine. We had put so much money into Chihango, preparing for new teams and street children. It was a melancholy sight to see long lines of children moving bed frames—so expensive to buy and transport—across the grass into our storage container.

On that last day Chihango never looked more beautiful. It was bright and breezy, the clouds so awe-inspiring behind our stately rows of rustling eucalyptus trees. As sunset drew near, and as I remembered all the power and joy we had experienced there, I understood that God had placed us where we wanted to be—at the battle line between heaven and hell. How could responsible men bring such cruelty on these children? But we knew our story in Mozambique was far from finished. Our King, the Creator of the universe, was still our loving heavenly Father; He would have His way in the end, and we would exult in Him.

To get out of Chihango, our staff worked day and night packing up and cleaning out building after building. In the rain and mud, and until three and four o'clock in the morning, they loaded our trucks and trailer and hauled our belongings to storage in Maputo wherever friends offered us space. All of us had only one place to go at first: our little office flat in Maputo, which had a bit of a patio, a crowded garage and a laundry workroom in the back.

We were inundated by our very most needy children, the youngest street orphans with absolutely no relatives or friends to whom they could go. They had walked barefoot fifteen miles into the city and streamed into our flat. They told us they had been beaten with large sticks for singing. They said they would go where we go because they were going to worship the Lord. When I told them we had no place for them, their simple reply was, "But, Mama, you said there would always be enough!"

What could I say? They kept piling in, maybe a hundred of them. We stuffed bunk beds in our dilapidated little garage full of grease and cobwebs. Loaned army cots were all over our yard and driveway. Urine ran in our hallway. We hosed the kids down to try to wash them. All our doors and windows were full of faces!

We didn't know how to cope. We had nowhere near the food or the cooking and sanitation facilities we needed. Boxes, clothes and suitcases were piled high everywhere. Everyone was totally exhausted; everything was in complete chaos. And more children kept gravitating to our gate. We ran out of strength, crying as we watched our sea of faces gather. I wondered seriously, even after Toronto, "Does God really care? What is He like anyway?" I never thought He would leave us in a situation like this.

Our daughter, Crystalyn, began to cry because she was so hungry. I thought I was going to snap. We didn't have any big pans for cooking. We weren't prepared in any way to feed all those children. A precious woman from the U.S. embassy came over with food. "I brought you chili and rice for your family!" she announced sweetly, with just enough for the four of us. We hadn't eaten in days. I opened a door and showed her all our children. "I have a big family!" I pointed out tiredly but in complete and desperate earnest. My friend got serious. "There's not enough! I need to go home and cook some more!" But I just asked her to pray over the food. Now she was upset. "Don't do this!" she begged. But she prayed, quickly. I got out the plastic plates we used for street outreaches, and also a small pot of cornmeal I had. We began serving, and right from the start I gave everyone a full bowl. I was dazed and overwhelmed. I barely understood at the time what a wonderful thing was happening. But all our children ate, the staff ate, my friend ate and even our family of four ate. Everyone had enough.

Since then we have never said no to an orphaned, abandoned or dying child. Now we feed and take care of more than one thousand children. They eat and drink all they want of the Lord's goodness. Because He died, there is always enough.

Chapter 4

See Them One by One

Our eviction from Chihango left us and our more than three hundred children suddenly homeless. With nowhere else to meet, we gathered under trees in a beautiful, wind-swept field a mile from Chihango. Tears flowed freely all around as we remembered our times together and all that God had done among us, and as we interceded brokenly for the children. But our kids had learned. The Holy Spirit had taught them, and they would lay hands on us and comfort us. "Don't worry, Mama Aida," they would say to me. "Jesus will take care of us!" And He did.

We built thatched huts for our older boys on land quickly donated by local villagers. Two mission agencies offered us temporary emergency housing and daily school lessons for a limited number of children as long as we provided food, fuel, supplies, clothes and supervision. Then a fervent Christian and leading councilman of Matola, a nearby town outside Maputo, donated fifty acres of land to us in the country district of Machava. Thrilled to help us, he made us feel welcome and wanted. He said, "This is what Mozambique needs, and giving you land is the least we can do!"

We bought used army tents for dorms. For months we carried water from a mile away on a cart pulled by a donkey. The ground was sandy and full of worms and snakes, but the children didn't complain. We needed a place to meet, so I went off to a camping store in South Africa and asked for a big circus tent to cover a thousand people. That was a rare, special-order item that took six months to make. But for some reason a big group had ordered such a tent and never picked it up, so it was available immediately. We just needed ten thousand dollars. That very day an anonymous donor in California put ten thousand dollars in our account, and I came back with a beautiful, blue-and-white striped tent that we used for years. There is always enough!

We kept improving Machava, our beautiful land covered with shady cashew trees. A visiting construction team built cement slabs under the tents. We dug a well with a simple hand pump that provided clean, cool water. Our children laughed, danced and cried with gratitude. "Look at what Jesus has done for us!" Soon we had a tent city, and nearly every day brought in more orphaned and abandoned children.

Children as young as five years old wander through Maputo in blackened rags, scavenging in dumps, cooking entrails from garbage cans, crashing out on cement pavements in the hot sun or huddling under cardboard in pouring rains. Every child we meet is desperate for a piece of bread, a bit of change, a smile or a touch of love. We see them and take them in one by one.

Jesus taught me to do this long before in Hong Kong. After preaching to crowds of thousands, I started to walk the back alleys of Kowloon, and Jesus opened my eyes. It was as if I was seeing for the first time. Old ladies huddled under bridges, lonely men dressed in plastic bags, addicts lying on the cement under trees. God expanded my heart and let me feel a small part of His intense compassion. It was incredible, for it was never ending. I canceled all our big meetings and began to work among the poor, becoming friends with them and reaching them one by one. His mercy and compassion are greater than we ever imagined. He has called us to be His hands extended. He has called us to stop for the dying man, the dying woman and the dying child. He has called us to see what He sees and to do what He does. And because He has called us to this, there is always enough of all that we need.

One day while praying I had a vivid vision. The wedding supper of the Lamb was all laid out. It was the most gorgeous food I had ever seen. The tables were exquisite, and they went on forever. I kept hearing the Lord say, "Wake up, Church! Wake up, Church! The feast is prepared, but the Church is not yet ready! The poor have not yet been called to the feast!"

And then I had a vision of Jesus and me dancing on the garbage dump in Maputo. In the vision Jesus was calling people to Himself. He was gathering youth and children dressed in filthy rags, blackened by the soot of burning garbage, with festering sores and bloated bellies. As we touched each person one by one, they were completely healed. Their bellies became flat. Their sores were cured. They were made clean. As He and I stopped for each one, He would put beautiful robes on them. Each one was different—red, blue, purple, gold and silver. We began to lead them in a dance out of the dump to the wedding feast. It was the most beautiful place, pure and clean, filled by His presence. He took each child by the hand and sat them at the head table.

Because of that vision I started working in the *bocaria,* a massive garbage dump outside Maputo. It is, to the human eye, a desperate place where the poorest of the poor make their homes. They scrounge for food and search through refuse to find anything they can use or sell. Many children live in this dump right among the swarming flies and in the smoldering garbage and indescribable stench. They are covered with skin infections and bloated with worms. It is a most difficult place to minister for many of our visitors, and it is impossible to prepare anyone fully for the assault on the senses that he will experience there. The uninitiated are overwhelmed by so much filth and nauseating wretchedness. But to me it is one of the most beautiful places on earth. The people are hungry for Jesus. They want Him. They want His friendship. They run to Him and depend on Him. They make Jesus smile.

God has done wonders at the dump. During our first visits

some of the youth threatened to kill us. Yelling and waving broken bottles at us, they vowed to slit our throats. They were drunk and stoned on any drugs they could find that pharmacies had thrown out. All I could do was remember my vision of Jesus touching them, loving them, healing them and inviting them to the wedding feast.

I told the guys about the vision. Immediately some of the roughest ones fell to their knees in tears and were saved. They were still rough, but now they protected us.

People abandon their kids at the dump because they can't feed them. Nina, a little eleven-year-old girl, was left there, and she began to live with us off and on. She had been raped many times and, when we found her, was afflicted with gonorrhea, syphilis, AIDS and tuberculosis all at the same time. God has healed her of tuberculosis, and she is beginning to open up to the pure love being poured out upon her. She loves Jesus and loves to worship. As we walk among our friends in the dump, they are being healed and set free. When I first started sharing in the dump, no one had any idea who Jesus was. Several of the guys said, "He sounds really nice! Can you please bring Him here so we can talk to Him?"

Not one person in the garbage dump has said no to an invitation to meet Jesus. They are all hungry for the Bread of Life. We started our dump church in a tiny, blackened shell of a building, and it's one of my favorite churches in the whole world. We sing, preach and worship in eye-stinging smoke. Our arms are black with swarms of flies. Broken glass and garbage are all over the floor. We put thatch over a rusty overhead frame to make it more bearable in the sun. Barefoot, wrinkled old ladies from the community sit on the floor and clap for joy, their smiles breaking out at every glorious testimony. Children and teenagers crowd in on the sides, many crying on their faces in repentance or worshiping with hands high. Many are diseased and hungry, and some know they will die within weeks, but they are thrilled to find their Savior.

We bring doctors and nurses here. We bring preachers here. We bring every visitor here. I always give Communion when I come, and Jesus meets us with His rich presence. Each week we help the people build new houses out of reeds and tin roofing in the surrounding area, always a very exciting miracle to them. And more children climb in our truck to come live with us. Jesus is dancing with us on the garbage dump. He is with us reaching out His hands of love to the broken and abandoned. He cares.

After the dump, the streets of downtown Maputo are my favorite place to pray with people. When I met Helena, she was a prostitute, a maimed, malnourished, twelve-year-old child forced by poverty to sell her body on the streets. Years before, the reed hut she shared with her grandmother and brothers caught fire and burned down. She was so badly burned that one leg was actually burned off. I could see her scarred knee where her leg ended. Helena survived the fire, but because she was disabled, her grandmother decided she was of no use. She had become a burden to her family, and the decision was made to kill her. Helena's brothers were instructed to take her out to a field and stone her.

They dragged her to the field and threw rocks at her until she passed out. Assuming she was dead, they left her. A man walking through the field discovered her, severely injured and unconscious, but alive. He picked her up and took her to the hospital. In such cases the government hospital is free. Helena spent six months there recovering, and during her entire stay she didn't have one visitor.

I found Helena one night during our street outreach. I told her of my Father God's love and forgiveness. I told her what Jesus did for her. She fell apart in my arms and wept. She asked me over and over, "Jesus would do that for me? Jesus would die for me? That is so beautiful. That is so lovely. I want to know Him and follow Him." That night on the street Helena came home to live with us.

God began to do a deep healing in her heart. She went through a lot of deliverance. Her family was deeply into witchcraft. Once she was set free from demonic influence, she was completely transformed. This young girl who had endured so much hardship, trauma, ridicule and abuse was now consumed by the great love of God. She was indebted to Him. Her immediate reaction was, "He has forgiven me for so much. He has set me free. I forgive my grandmother and my brothers. I want to go and tell them about the love of God."

Helena has risked her life to go back to the family who had tried to murder her so that she could share God's love with them. She has returned to her home three times. She was not received well, but she refuses to give up. Her grandmother is still very strongly involved with the occult and hasn't responded. One of her brothers has disappeared, but the other one is listening. Helena continues to pray for her family every day.

One of our volunteers made her a simple but functioning prosthesis. It gives her the ability to stand on her own without her crutch. When she wears a long Mozambican skirt her leg is barely noticeable. Helena, now fifteen years old, is one of the most anointed intercessors in our church and leads the girls' worship team.

One night I met Ernesto and took him home from the streets, where he had lived since he was six. Now he was twelve. He had been raped many times. After he had been with us for a while, he was taken up to heaven in a vision. He danced with angels, and they put him on their shoulders. They kept dancing with him, bouncing up and down as they sang one of our well-known and energetic African songs. The angels took him to the throne of God and placed him on the Lord's lap. The Lord began to speak to him with great love and emotion, saying, "Stop what you are doing. I care about your suffering and brought you to this center." Jesus told him not to insult or hit other people. He said He wanted to use him as a pastor, and that He would use him to do miracles. He would pray for the blind and they would see again. He was told to pray a lot and that one day he would find his family. He was not to be afraid because when Jesus died, He was not afraid. "Don't forget me," Jesus said, "and always remember that I have saved you."

One day when Ernesto was sick, Jesus told him to pray, and when he did he saw many angels. He sang together with them with all his heart, and then they took him to heaven again. He heard, "You are saved and you are healed!" He was brought to Jesus, who told him He was coming back to earth. After Jesus healed him, he was told to tell the Church his story. Jesus told him to preach in the community and not to forget to read the Bible. Ernesto says, "I am obeying!"

We wrote down other testimonies and sent out news all during this time as our children's center grew, and we will include here some excerpts:

July 1997
Seven more children from the streets of Maputo found a home with us last week at our camp of army tents on our new land. None of them is sure how old he is, but the boys are between eight and ten. They've been on their own for years, hardened and skilled at survival through begging, stealing and "guarding" cars. Today they testified at our Sunday morning worship service, and each radiated glory and grace from Jesus Himself. What a joy to see them so happy!

One little boy, Lulu, told us, "I know Jesus loves me because He gave me this family and this place to live, and if Jesus loves me, then He loves everyone!" There was Sheila, a girl who is maybe seventeen, mentally retarded and hardly able to speak. While on the streets she heard that we would help her somehow, and she managed to get to our office gate in town. She was thin and in rags, cold and so very sad. She hated living on the streets and prostituting herself. We promised to take her out to our center, and she waited patiently and silently until we could go. We could hardly imagine how much she had suffered. But today, after a week at the center, her eyes were bright and she could not stop smiling. Yes, she's so happy now, she told us. She loves Jesus and is a different person! The others were also bubbling with joy, even as they told their grim histories. They could not contain their relief and pleasure at finding a brand-new life in the Lord with our family of children—all rescued from excruciating, poverty-stricken circumstances.

August 1998
The children have been especially touched by the Holy Spirit in recent weeks. Our staff tells us that the children's hearts have been "marked" by the Lord, and there is a new spirit of gentleness, love and cooperation among them. The children are praying for each other and getting healed. God is granting dreams and visions daily.

One little boy, Paul, was transformed overnight when Jesus came to him in a dream and told him to stop his stealing and misbehavior. He prayed the most beautiful and urgent prayer in church the next day and powerfully exhorted the other children to leave their sins and follow Jesus. Amelia, one of our housemothers for the little children, found herself in a vision, standing in a mighty, refreshing river, filled to overflowing with the joy of the Lord. Children who have experienced the most abuse and pain in their pasts are now laughing with joy and free of evil spirits that have oppressed them. Sheila, for example, who is retarded, can hardly speak and is pregnant as a result of a rape that occurred when she briefly ran away, is free and filled with peace. Through the Holy Spirit she prays with beauty and anointing, once quoting the Lord's Prayer in perfect Portuguese.

Our children are discovering the glory of feeling the direct touch of God on their hearts and even their bodies. We just baptized another 29 children after three months of teaching, and each one was filled with the Spirit and prayed in tongues after coming up out of the water identified with Jesus! Some were overcome with joy in the water, and I could hardly stand, laughing and crying with gratitude to the Lord that such as these would be granted His presence.

And then came attacks, all in one day. After a beautiful service at the dump where the presence of the Holy Spirit was strong, troublemakers started a riot at the bread distribution. Katie, one of our staff missionaries, was cut, and I was hit in the face. Later that day our newest truck was rear-ended and badly damaged by a lady who totaled her car in the accident. That night the same truck was shot up by bandits as it was driven by Joel Skjonsby, who had his wife, Janet, and son Jeff with him. A 45-caliber bullet missed Jeff by inches. Joel and his family gave up their vacation to minister with us in Africa, and we have been hugely blessed by their labor of love and willingness to lay down their lives for Jesus.

The attacks continued. My truck window was smashed, and bags were stolen. Another truck caught on fire dangerously. Our project engineer's truck was hijacked. Jesse, our Brazilian director at Machava, came down with serious malaria, as did Rolland the month before. I ended up in the hospital with an unknown virus, and Janet also went in with pneumonia. Then three hundred people at Machava were out of water when our well pump broke down . . . .

Our daily work is filled with frustrations and delays from operating in such a poor environment, a feature of life here that especially impacts visiting teams. Many come wanting to work quickly and energetically, making the most of their time. Instead, they are confronted by supply, communication and transportation problems that are the common lot of the underdeveloped world. But God is breaking hearts, enlarging them and preparing them for His use as He sees fit anywhere in the world. We never waste time when we throw away our lives for His sake, wanting only Him and His Spirit in us. He is not daunted and deterred in the least by any of our troubles, and by faith in Him we overcome. He knows the way forward; He will lead us. May we reflect His glory as we participate in His nature!

January 1999
It was a night like most on the streets of the capital city of one of the world's poorest countries. Our friends were resting on cardboard boxes. Smoke from burning garbage made it difficult to see. Rotting food added stench to the hot, humid air of our December summer. My street friends lined up to greet me, and one by one they would tell me of their sicknesses and ask for prayer. Zacharias and Dino, who lived on the streets for years before moving to our center at Zimpeto,

prayed alongside me with love and faith. They remember what it is like to spend long days and nights alone without a friendly word.

I asked about people I had prayed for the week before, and my friends would lead me to them past many more fires, around corners and down alleys. Francisco was lying in the dark on garbage, laboring to breathe. He brightened when he saw us, and eagerly showed us his hand. It was paralyzed the week before, and now he could begin to move it. He was so grateful, and received more prayer. His ten-year-old son, Felipe, was with him, and also fights to survive on the streets. We found another lonely man in the dark from South Africa who was thrilled to be invited to eat, sing and pray with us at our street meeting. Felipe came along and brought back dinner for his father—after he gave his heart to Jesus and prayed to his heavenly Father!

We talked to and prayed with many this night, and so importantly we stopped, waited and listened to our friends, letting them tell their stories. God's treasures in Maputo are precious to us and to Him . . . .

Last Sunday in church Manuel got up in front of hundreds of people and fearlessly shared his vision. He saw a dove descend down over us, and as fire breathed from its mouth we all fell to the ground. Then the voice of Jesus called out, "Many still do not know Me and are not saved. I stand at the door and knock. Now is the time to open your hearts to Me, for I am coming soon! Manuel, you must go back to your people and preach to them!" And then Rabia spoke of seeing various fields, some fertile and ripe with grain, and others rocky and crawling with snakes. A teenager from the dump saw himself in a dark, muddy pit, and then saw us pulling him out into the bright light and onto a straight road.

These and other of our young men and women who are receiving revelations are new to the Scriptures and the things of God. They do not know about the Holy Spirit dove, Jesus standing at the door and knocking, the parable of the sower, the miry pit in the Psalms, etc., and they ask us innocently, "What do these things mean?" And, of course, we tell them!

Evan had a vision in which angels took him up to heaven, and together they all sat around Jesus, worshiping Him and singing together. Jesus gave him strong words to take back to his friends at our center. Evan got louder and bolder and delivered his prophetic message to all our children. Jesus is coming soon, very soon, but many of us are not ready. We must all make a choice between fire and heaven, and we must not rob and take drugs anymore. We must get ready! Jesus wants to live in clean bodies and hearts. And then Jesus told Evan that he, too, must go back to earth and preach the Gospel in Mozambique. Today he is a leader in our street churches.

One Sunday on the way to church, Thomasito suddenly cried out, "Look! There's an angel beside the truck!" Other children see Jesus in meetings and in their dorm rooms. Always He tells them, "I'm coming, much sooner than you think! Get ready!"

We found Aldelto living on the streets near the central hospital. He was used to beating and robbing people, and he was afflicted with epilepsy. Norberto, one of our older boys, persuaded him to come to our center, where he received Jesus wholeheartedly. Today he is healed of epilepsy and wants to be a preacher!

Ernesto, a nine-year-old, was on the streets a long time. He was always beating and stealing, too, and he especially tried to steal everything he could out of churches. He would show up at our outreaches and mock us, telling everyone to go away. Already he smoked, drank and took drugs. Finally, he got saved and came to our center, and now his heart is set on attending our Bible school and becoming a preacher also.

Amardelsa lived at home, and his mother took him to church, but he stole everything he could and got into so much trouble that he ran away. He came to one of our street outreaches, and Jesus changed his whole life. Adelio also was living at home, but he got beaten so much that he ran away. On the streets he kept stealing, and he eventually stole what was for him a great deal of money from his own mother. Street friends told him to buy a bicycle with it, but instead he got cigarettes, beer and glue to inhale. Christians on the street told him to come to an outreach, which he did. He met Jesus, and now he plans to approach his mother for forgiveness.

Arleta's mother wanted her killed as a baby. Eventually her mother disappeared, and as Arleta grew up, her father's friends would beat and rape her as they passed her around. They even forced her to eat her own vomit. Finally she fled to the streets where we found her—and she found Jesus! Today she glows with the Holy Spirit, and she has found and forgiven her father. She still doesn't know where her mother is.

April 1999
Demons put up a struggle, as they usually do here. Many of our children come from backgrounds where witchcraft is practiced seriously, and some have been thrown out of their homes for coming to Jesus. Curses are put on them for having anything to do with us, and we have had to comfort and pray with little ones whose relatives never want to see them again. Demons often manifest at baptisms, but after gentle prayer they go, and the children come up out of the water free and filled with joy, often speaking in tongues. This last time a demon almost drowned a child, but Jesus prevailed again.

Our children laugh and play without a care—such a contrast to their previous lives alone and lost. They rise early to sing and pray. Always looking for ways to help, and always running to us with affection and enthusiasm, they model for us what it means to be childlike in Jesus. We watch them to learn all we can about what Jesus is looking for in us! And He enjoys their company, for weekly, almost daily, they come to us with their testimonies of dreams and visions in which they meet the Lord and are shown heavenly realms. And as He visits them, they change; they become radically serious about serving Him with their lives and about cleaning impurities out of their hearts. They stand up and testify, shyly at first, and then strongly and boldly as they continue. They will preach, even while still young, and they will be called "oaks of righteousness, a planting of the Lord for the display of his splendor."

Last week we again took some notes of their testimonies. One little girl, Vera Rosinha, six years old, was joined by Jesus and an angel as she prayed simply. Others, like Rainha Fernando, twelve, are shown vividly how Jesus saved them from Satan, the vicious killer. Moises Sitoe, a teenager of fifteen, saw a hundred angels climbing and descending on a stairway to heaven, all singing, "Glory to God!" Edgas Gove, ten, was given a Bible by a big angel in a dream. Paulo Machava, thirteen, found himself singing and dancing with an angel. Often Jesus and the angels sing with them the very same songs they learn from us down here!

In spite of the extreme stresses and chaos that result from diving into the arena of the poor and desperate, we sense that Jesus is pleased and that He is with us in spite of our weaknesses. We are encouraged by your responses, by the beautiful intercession continuing in many places on our behalf and especially by the way the King Himself comes to our "insignificant" kids. They are treasures to Him and have become treasures to us. They speak sermons and volumes about what is important to God.

August 1999
[Maria]: "I was in the tent church and I saw a great, white, brilliant light. The Holy Spirit came to me and took me with Him to heaven. We went to see Jesus. He sat on a very big chair, and I received His love. Later in the vision I went to the beach with Davidinho, and when we went into the water Davidinho began to speak, play and walk!" [Davidinho is one of our little boys who suffered brain damage recently from cerebral malaria and meningitis. Although Davidinho was brain-dead for months, now he is perfectly healthy and happy in Jesus!]

[Isabel]: "I cried and cried when I prayed. I saw Mama Aida and Fabricio. An angel took us to heaven. I said, 'Jesus, I'm a sinner!' And He said, 'My daughter, I have forgiven all your sins.' I came back and the church was full of water, clear and bright. All the people asked where the water was from, and I knew it was from the Holy Spirit. Jesus wants to do a miracle with this water!"

Many like Isabel have seen in visions a river or body of water on our property, blessing and healing all who enter it. It is a foretaste of "the river of the water of life, as clear as crystal, flowing from the throne of God" (Revelation 22:1), and "where the river flows everything will live" (Ezekiel 47:9).

We are "treasure hunting" in the dump and on the streets, looking for each and every desperate child. Jesus is never out of resources, and He never stops providing for the kind of work that excites Him. We always want to be ready to join Him in doing what is in His heart. Our staff often gets frustrated with me, and we all get overwhelmed over and over, but we can never go backwards. I can never deny the vision I received. And always, after we lose all faith in ourselves and only see His face, there is enough.

Chapter 5

Explosion!

Now in Africa we were seeing the sequel to the revival Rolland's grandfather saw among his orphans in China. That was not an isolated outpouring with no further fruit. In it Rolland and I saw the heart of God. We saw how He feels about the lost and forgotten. We saw how He delights to use the helpless and hopeless to accomplish His best work. We saw His pleasure in revealing Himself to those humble and poor in spirit enough to appreciate Him. We saw His ability to use simple children to ignite revival. Now we were seeing Him do the same thing in Mozambique. And what He was doing in our children's center fired our appetite all the more for revival.

We were simply desperate for more of God. The children's visions were really encouraging, but we wanted to see an entire nation come to God. Rolland and I so loved the manifest presence of God that we longed to be wherever He was pouring out His Spirit. Whenever a speaking invitation brought us to the States, we figured we were close enough to make the trip back to Toronto. In January of 1998, Randy Clark was there preaching about the apostolic anointing, laying down our lives and the holy fire of God. He pointed to me and said, "God is asking, 'Do you want Mozambique?'" I experienced the heavenly fire of God falling on me. I was so hot I literally thought I was going to burn up and die. I remember crying out, "Lord,

I'm dying!" I heard the Lord clearly speak to my heart, "Good, I want you dead!" He wanted me completely emptied of self so He could pour even more of His Spirit into my life.

For seven days I was unable to move. Rolland had to pick me up and carry me. I had to be carried to the washroom, to the hotel and back to the meeting. The weight of His glory was upon me. I felt so heavy I could not lift my head. Some passing by thought it was funny to see someone stuck to the floor for so long. If I was put in a chair, I would slide off onto the floor again. I was utterly and completely helpless. I was unable to speak for most of the seven days. This holy, fearful, awesome presence of God completely changed my life. I've never been so humbled, never felt so poor, so helpless, so vulnerable. I even needed help to drink water. There was nothing funny about it. It was a most holy time. I learned more in those seven days than in ten years of academic theological study.

The Lord spoke to me about relinquishing control to Him. He showed me the importance of the Body of Christ. It had taken us seventeen years to plant four churches, and two of them were pretty weak. As I lay there engulfed in His presence, He spoke to me about hundreds of churches being planted in Mozambique. I remember laughing hysterically, thinking I would have to live to be two hundred years old before that promise was fulfilled!

God showed me that I needed to learn to work with the rest of the Body. He put Ephesians 4 on my heart: "As a prisoner for the Lord, then, I urge you to live a life worthy of the calling you have received. Be completely humble and gentle; be patient, bearing with one another in love. Make every effort to keep the unity of the Spirit through the bond of peace. There is one body and one Spirit—just as you were called to one hope when you were called—one Lord, one faith, one baptism; one God and Father of all, who is over all and through all and in all" (Ephesians 4:1–6).

I was a type-A, driven person, and God had to break and humble me. He showed me my total inadequacy to do anything in my own strength. Being unable to move for seven days drove the point home as nothing else could have ever done. I remember several times hearing people whisper with pity that I was crippled, a quadriplegic. I never liked being dependent on others. I have been a leader as long as I can remember. My mother told me that even as a young child I used to line up all the preschoolers and lead them around. God had to remove so much of me from me so that He could do something in and through me.

I thought I had been depending on Him to plant churches, when in reality I depended a lot on my own abilities. Naturally, things moved pitifully slowly. It's comical to think we can do God's work for Him. It's all grace. He allows us to participate with Him, and so there is always enough. He showed me how much I needed Him and the Body of Christ. He is calling us to complete humility and gentleness. It is never about us; it is always about Him. We need patience for every person we encounter in ministry, that we can be long-suffering, bearing with one another in His love, able to love the unlovely.

He is our only hope. He is our Lord. Our faith is in Him. We are baptized into Him. We lay down our lives. We die to ourselves in baptism. We are raised new creations in Christ. God is calling each of us to walk in the mercy and grace He has given us. He prepares us for works of service. Do we see what He sees? Do we feel what He feels? Can we hear the cry of His heart for the lost? This is poverty of spirit. God is calling us to be poor in spirit. When we are poor in spirit, we no longer compete. We no longer jostle for titles. When we have no drive to be noticed and known, we are not offended by lack of attention. We find no satisfaction in ministry status. Then we can walk in unity, preferring others above ourselves. Our only desire is to live the life of a humble servant-lover of our Lord Jesus.

After that transforming experience, everything in my ministry changed. He brought me to a place of utter dependence on Him. When I returned to Mozambique I began releasing people in ministry. I began to recognize potential ministers even in children as young as eight. I began relinquishing control and delegating responsibilities. The Lord started bringing missionaries from many nations to help us. Young men and women were called into ministry from all over Mozambique. I saw that it wasn't important if I spoke, but that I could release others to fulfill their potential in God. As I became less and He became more, the ministry grew at a phenomenal rate.

In 1997 we had bought new property at Zimpeto, a northern district of Maputo. It was on a major highway with electric power lines, and we could develop it more fully than Machava. In faith we drew up a site plan, and a construction team from Hawaii helped us begin our first house. In early 1998 we moved our youngest children over from Machava and kept working on more dorms. Then came classrooms and housing for staff and visitors. Now, with two centers, we could handle even more children and have a better administrative base.

We moved our big tent from Machava to Zimpeto. The Holy Spirit fell on our meetings. Hearing of God's presence at Zimpeto, the hungry traveled down from the north to participate in our worship and ministry. Children and teenagers from the streets and the dump did everything they could to find transportation to our weekly tent meetings. Virtually all who came, maybe a hundred a week, gave their hearts to Jesus. They would seek Him earnestly on their faces in the dirt and heat, knowing that He is what they have always needed and wanted.

At the time we wrote:

We meet in our big tent, dirty and ripped from so much use. We sit on old, surplus army benches, many broken, bent and rusted. Rain and wind come and go. Dust clouds the air as we all sing and dance. We are soaked with perspiration. At night we see dimly by the light of one or two intermittent fluorescent tubes. But Jesus loves to be here, and more than anything we want to repent before Him, see His beauty and make Him feel loved and wanted. May God Himself be thrilled as He senses the incense of worship rise up from our faraway, simple worship center where our only wealth is the Holy Spirit!

And again:

> Daybreak at Zimpeto brings to our ears the purest sound we know: simple children singing praises to Jesus with all their hearts. Even with us, they are still so poor. They have one or two changes of clothes and almost no possessions. They eat with their fingers. They play in the dirt. Their school is a hut with a thatched roof. And they love each other. They smile, laugh and jump with excitement. They are on their way to heaven, and they know it. They are safe in Jesus, and they feel loved. And so they are among the richest people on earth!

For twenty years Rolland and I had prayed to see the Kingdom of God unfold before our eyes like this. Jesus reveals Himself to these children. They dance with angels in visions and are taken to see the King on His throne. They intercede on their faces for the nation of Mozambique. They testify fearlessly before street gangs and government ministers. They are a key part of God's solution for the poorest country on earth!

God was with us and began making an impact at the highest levels of Mozambique's government through our children. Top officials have seen developmental projects and aid programs, but seeing the love of God poured out on those least likely to receive help of any kind brought them to tears as they visited our center. We received offers of cooperation, even from the president's office, instead of the cold indifference and even hostility we had come to expect from governmental departments.

Local churches and pastors were touched by the children's center, too. They saw the love and mercy of God "fleshed out," and they were encouraged. Through the ministry there, we came in touch with evangelists and leaders who were also fired with desire for revival. We met Surpresa Sithole, an amazing Mozambican evangelist whose father was a witch doctor. With an audible voice God had called Surpresa out of his demonic household and with frequent visions and revelations had led him through years of hardships until he was pioneering and leading churches all over central Mozambique. Through Surpresa ninety of these churches asked us in 1998 if they could join our ministry and come under our leadership and supervision. We registered our churches with the government as Comunhao na Colheita ("Community in Harvest" in Portuguese) and cried out to the Lord, asking how we should shepherd such a movement.

That year on one trip Rolland traveled three thousand miles to visit many of these mostly rural churches located deep in the African bush. Driving hours a day over tortuous trails by four-wheel-drive truck, hiking for endless miles and even canoeing up rivers past crocodiles, he and Surpresa preached to destitute village people becoming rich in faith. The Holy Spirit moved out across the countryside of Mozambique, where seventy percent of its people live, and where the traditional churches of the towns do not venture.

I went north soon afterward and taught at our first conference of pastors in the central city of Beira. I prophesied, exhorted and preached my heart out to these simple pastors with so little training, and the Holy Spirit fell on them. Usually fearful of the government, they were amazed at the favor granted us after our early struggles at Chihango in the south. They could not get enough teaching and longed for us to visit them.

We started a Bible school at Zimpeto to equip national pastors, right among our children. We simply set up school desks in the central area of one of our dorms. Our classroom was hot, crowded and not always very clean or fresh, but heaven touched down. No hardships were enough to keep them from the things of God. Many had to leave their wives and children with precariously meager supplies, but they threw their cares on Jesus and came anyway with huge spiritual hunger. They came for three months at a time, with the intention of returning once a year for three more years. We only brought 12 pastors down for our first session, but then it was 50, and then 90, then 120 and more. They rose at four in the morning to pray and worship loudly for hours. They filled our altars at every meeting. They drank in everything we could teach them. They burned with zeal. And when they returned to their villages, nothing could stop them from carrying the wildfire of the Holy Spirit to other villages all around.

Pastor Rego is one of these pastors, ministering in Dondo, just outside Beira in Sofala Province. He is well acquainted with poverty and hunger. He lives in a grass and mud hut, working diligently for the Kingdom, unconcerned with material rewards. His sole desire is to see the lost come to Jesus. He is well aware of his own limitations, yet he has seen miracles that the prosperous Church only dreams about.

At the end of one of our sessions, I prophesied to Rego and one other pastor, Joni, that they would be raising the dead. I exhorted them to start praying for every dead person they saw.

Pastor Rego was obedient to that word. He has completely laid down his life for the Master's service, and you can see the passion of God in his eyes as he tells his story:

> Our country is now in a situation where there are no jobs. Many people cannot afford to go to a hospital or anywhere else. The only place they can go is to the church. They have no money for a doctor. My church was a new, struggling work. I started it in my house. People said, "No one will come to your church—they will go to a more beautiful church." God gave me a vision and said, "Do this work and I will bring the people to your church."
>
> I open the Bible and do what it says. When people see a miracle in the church, there is a lot more growth. When you do miracles they say, "We are in the times of the Bible!" I tell the people why they are healed. It is the proof that God is alive. And they go and tell other people.
>
> When I saw the first major miracle in my church, it really grew. I had a lot more power in my ministry when a mother was raised from the dead. And every day the sick people come and they are healed, and they go away and tell others.
>
> A missionary built very close to our church, but he has left because no one went to his church. He made *mahaya* [a drink

Mozambicans love, made out of cornmeal], and he cooked for all the Christians, hoping to bring them in with the things he could offer. But they came to the church where the miracles were.

We don't have anything to give to people that would attract them, but we saw more happening than he could ever give. People left the food and drink so they could come to our church and be healed. And so our church is growing very quickly. We are walking in the ways of the Bible.

There are churches that have people who call themselves prophets, but it is very different from the way we do it. They tell people they have to get milk or water from the ocean to be healed. We just open the Bible and speak about what Jesus did, and we do that, too. The disciples did the same thing. Then we pray for the sick, and all the evil spirits leave. The people prefer to come, because they receive the power of God.

Recently I was with my brothers in the Lord from the church. We felt God call us to pray and fast for three days with no water or food. The second night of our fast somebody came to my house. It is beside the church, so he saw us in the church. It was Amelia, the secretary of the district, and he told me his wife died. I went with him, leaving my wife and some others to organize things for the next day.

When we got to his house, everyone was crying. I went inside. His wife's head was covered already. Suddenly I felt something touch me. I thought, "Oh, God, I need to pray now for you to give me the power to do a miracle." I remember Peter did miracles. I'd like to be like Peter. Who said we can't do this, too? So I got up. I started to feel strength and great power coming into me.

I told everyone to be quiet and not cry anymore, because this mother who died is a Christian. We need to ask the Lord to forgive our sins. Nobody wanted to be quiet. I asked again, "Please be quiet now. Calm down." They wanted to keep crying and feel sad, but eventually they were quiet.

We sang and worshiped the Lord. Then my friend Francisco, one of our counselors, also started to feel the power of God.

I got next to this dead mother. I took the cover off her head and began to pray. I prayed for over an hour. She was very cold. The second hour I started to feel warmth coming into her. I could feel her body warming up. I prayed all the way down her body. When I got down to her legs, the bottom of her legs were still cold.

I picked her up, and then her eyes were open. She began to vomit and vomit. I can't even explain it. She spat up white sputum, white and yellow vomit.

I told a woman, "Sit here and hold her," because she could see everybody now. "Let's keep praying," I said. Her legs were beginning to get warm. We prayed some more. The third hour her whole body had movement. She was alive!

Some men wanted to take her to the hospital that night. I said, "No. Why didn't you take her to the hospital when she was dead? Why would you take her now? Don't you know? Let's go to church! Look! Look! She is alive."

There was a lot of confusion. Then I started to get worried, and I prayed I would have strength for the church. God wanted to show His glory, and I didn't know if He would show His glory and then take her away again. I was afraid of her dying again.

She couldn't speak. A little girl in our church said, "My mother has to go to church! If she goes to the hospital she will die!" Nobody said a word. The people knew God had put words in the little girl's mouth. So we took her and carried her to church. It was Saturday, and we spent the whole night in prayer. She began to speak.

The neighbors and friends who didn't know she was raised from the dead had gone to work to get the day off because she had died. When they came back, there was no dead body. They were told, "Oh, she's in church!" They said, "Why? Is she alive?" "Yes, she is alive!"

So they all came to church. Her husband was converted right away. On Sunday after the message, everybody took this mother back to her house. Our church is full now! This is a wonderful miracle in our church that helped it to grow. She had died of AIDS. When she went to the hospital, she was rejected because of her AIDS. But now she is alive! I called yesterday—she is still alive! Her five children are in the church, and all her extended family.

God has also raised the dead through Pastor Joni, whose church is near Chimoio, farther up the highway toward Zimbabwe. One night Tanneken, one of our staff missionaries in the north, and I were ministering to Joni's little congregation in their humble mud-and-thatch church. A lady named Rosa, mother of six, jumped up with excitement at seeing me. "You're the one I saw in my vision!" she cried. She shook and shouted as she poured out her testimony to me. She had been gravely sick with cholera, and as she lay dying she saw Pastor Joni and me in a vision. She begged her husband, "If and when I die, go get Pastor Joni!"

At about 1:00 A.M. she did die, and her husband went off to find their pastor. Joni was tired but came anyway. He sang, worshiped and prayed for hours, even as Rosa's family stood by crying. As dawn arrived, Rosa began to move, and then crawl—and then she got up and ate rice! "I was taken up to heaven," she said, "and I saw this huge gate. But a voice told me I couldn't go in yet. It wasn't my time and I had to go back." So now Rosa is a worshiper, passionate about Jesus. And Joni came down to a pastors' conference in Maputo and told the story with fire and conviction.

Others have also been raised from the dead. For the first time in my life I (Heidi) saw totally blind eyes, white from cataracts, change color and become normal and healthy. We do our best to preach the Word clearly, and as signs and wonders follow, the remotest and most forgotten of the African bush are being added to the Church. By the end of 1999, we had two hundred churches in the countryside, and I saw a vision of four hundred churches by the following year. Our dusty, plain, little center for street children had become a center of revival for the whole country.

At the time we could not have imagined what God would

allow next. Mozambique was brought to its knees by the worst flooding in living memory. In reaching out to flood victims with the love of God, we saw an outcry for the things of God that exceeded all our prophetic foresight and expectations. Since then the people of this poor land have surged toward the Savior, and we are thrilled to tell the story.

Chapter 6

Floods in Mozambique

In February of 2000, the floods came. Rain pounded on our tin and asbestos roofs at Zimpeto for days. Thunder boomed all night. Torrents of running water carved deep gullies in our property. Rooms were flooded, leaks were everywhere, the power went out.

Then we got a call from our Machava property a half-hour away, where almost two hundred of our older children stayed. Our land was completely flooded and everyone had to evacuate. Jesse and Racquel, our Brazilian directors there, led the children out on foot down dirt roads roaring with floodwaters, mud and debris, often descending waist and shoulder deep through the currents.

They hiked for several hours as we struggled to meet them with our available trucks and pick up as many as possible. The main roads were cut off. Concrete was torn away and turned into raging rapids. For a while it looked like we could not reach them at all. But finally with local guides we found alternate routes over side roads, got our four-wheel-drive trucks in as deep as we dared and met up with a soaked band of children bringing nothing but the clothes on their backs.

Meanwhile, on all sides of us local people saw their huts swept away. They waded down the highway wherever they could, carrying bags, chairs, whatever they could save, not knowing where to go. There were no emergency services, no sound of choppers overhead, no police in sight, no help on the way that we knew of. We stared into the face of defenseless poverty.

We needed to be led by the King. Tribulation was on us, and we had to find His priorities. He was being drastic with us, and we responded by crying out, "Have Your way, Jesus! Have Your way with us to the uttermost! Give us a strategy for these people. Make the difference for these helpless people!"

A flood from hell

Mozambique suddenly became an even less likely showcase for the glory of God. The flood was brought by the country's heaviest rain in fifty years. Three-fourths of its usual annual rainfall fell in three days, creating floods that left half a million people homeless in this already pitifully poor country. In our capital city of Maputo alone, more than a hundred thousand people lost everything. Crops all over the country were ruined. Hundreds and hundreds of square miles of farmland near us were under water. Food supplies ran low and prices multiplied. Water supplies were contaminated. The whole population was threatened by widespread famine and epidemics.

Transportation arteries up and down the country were cut. Streets and property were damaged terribly. Whole neighborhoods lay in reeking, stagnant water, filled with sewage. Mosquitoes bred quickly, and the incidence of malaria jumped up. Water purification plants flooded and shut down without power. The central hospital in Maputo filled with patients, but there was no medicine. The World Health Organization warned that almost a million people risked infection by cholera and meningitis.

Newspapers said the country's development was set back for years. Its fragile infrastructure was devastated. Its major industrial factories near Maputo, which finally brought economic growth, were shut down. And more rain continued to pour heavily as new storms moved in from the Indian Ocean.

Maputo only had a few main roads, and some of them became such deep canyons in places that they may remain unused for years. We started making long detours to get to town and from one center to the other. The many thousands who lost their homes and property around us crowded into schools, factories and warehouses wherever possible. Facilities were usually bare and broken down. Families sat on mats, surrounded by crates and buckets and the few things they could save and bring in sacks. We saw a few international aid agency trucks and personnel, but the refugees were mostly very hungry and without any idea what to do. Most needed medical attention.

Our Zimpeto property, where we lived ourselves and were building new dorms, was carved up and eroded by rushing currents, but not badly affected. Our larger Machava property was disastrously flooded. Water reached up to the windows of our church building. Our reed huts stood in pools of water. The rooms were a muddy mess, with debris strewn everywhere. Bugs and mosquitoes filled the air, and the water teemed with creatures. Local villagers stood in a lake to hand pump water from our valuable well.

I (Rolland) drove out there to speak to a remnant of our people staying behind to guard the property, and also our neighbors from the community. The waters had subsided after almost a week, but still I got my four-wheel-drive truck so deep that waves were washing over the hood, submerging the engine and choking off the air intake. Somehow I got the engine restarted with billows of smoke bubbling out of the water as we were sinking deeper into mud. Water was leaking through the doors and filling up the truck.

I got through, though, and preached from Romans 8— Nothing shall separate us from the love of God! It was wonderful to see the faith of our little orphan boys, our staff and even our visiting village ladies as they prayed and sang from their hearts, seated there under a tree on a spot of higher ground. I wanted the entire nation to trust God and taste His salvation as these did.

Our staff and the pastors in our Bible school went each day to different refugee camps, distributing bread, preaching and praying with everyone they could. The people all listened. They stood in long lines not only for bread, but also for tracts. They cried for prayer. Even the police jumped in to help us with distribution. Soon we were bringing bread to feed five thousand people in the homeless camps every day. In most places this was the only food they received from anyone.

It was very noticeable to me that the two most fervent of our pastors in this work, Rego and Joni, were the two who have seen the dead rise in their ministries up north. They were indefatigable, praying with compassion and excitement everywhere in each camp. They knew as few do that not even death is an impossible problem to our Lord and Savior.

Heaven in the dirt and rain

Even in such an intense, emergency atmosphere, our life with our children at Zimpeto continued on in Jesus. From my office, at the end of every day, I could hear their voices carry through the night air. Singing and shouting the praises of Jesus, they seemed oblivious to care. With our tent blown down and sagging into the swampy ground, we packed into our makeshift dining room for worship, tracking water and mud everywhere. Bugs crawled in our hair. We were all hot and wet with perspiration. When the power went off, we carried on against the roar of a generator. The kids danced up a storm before the Lord. They fell on their knees and faces to seek Him. Their hearts became gardens fit for the King. As we watched our children, we realized that God had chosen to take up residence in them right in front of our eyes, in the least likely circumstances we could imagine.

We were taking care of about seven hundred people daily at our own center, including our Mozambican staff, workers and students. And every day, even until late at night, the poor and desperate around us came for more—food, jobs, medicine, cement, money. We were crowded. Our hygiene was marginal. Our food was basic. We did the best we could medically. And still God chose to love us and show Himself, filling our community of faith with the good things of His Spirit.

The flooding continues

In March of 2000, President Chissano's secretary-general talked with us about his country's devastation. He had spent his life, he said, trying to help his country develop, once through communism, then through Mozambique's new democratic government and now through faith in Jesus as well. He loved our center and came there for a spiritual "bath." He wanted to be on our Mozambican board of directors. But he was in an emotional state. "How could God do this to our country?" he asked. "We've been knocked back fifty years!" More damage was done to Mozambique in three weeks of flooding than in 25 years of war.

We didn't know exactly, but we did know that in Jesus we always have reason to be positive, overwhelmingly and victoriously so. We thought Mozambique was enough of a challenge the way it was, but now we were in a position to see Jesus do much more than we expected. We could show that our faith in Him does overcome the world even in the most desperate situations. The question was, Did we want to be a part of God's work against extreme odds, or should we miss the glory and look away?

The flood was causing vastly more than homelessness. Corpses were floating in the floodwaters. Helicopters rescued ten thousand people from treetops and roofs along the Limpopo River, but ninety thousand more were stranded and in imminent danger of being swept away and drowned. Most could not swim, but the current was so powerful and deep that even strong swimmers could not last long. Each day those trapped in tiny areas grew weaker from hunger and exposure. Small children were affected quickly by malnutrition, so they were rescued first, leaving their parents behind.

Those rescued were deposited in isolated areas, still wet and miserable and without food or services of any kind. Children were hungry, sick and crying, with high fevers, and left without mothers and fathers. International aid was on the way but greatly delayed by red tape, and it was far less than what was required. In this huge country with so many orphans and children in distress, there were pitifully limited facilities for taking care of them. In the Lord we tried to fill a vacuum among the neediest of them all.

The flood kept rising, with more crests coming down the rivers from overflowing dams. Incredibly, another cyclone formed off Madagascar and headed toward Mozambique.

In Maputo we brought food and supplies daily to a cashew factory where we took responsibility for 3,000 refugees, and we also visited four or five other camps, one with 26,000 refugees. The UN World Food Program had food for that camp, but in many others there was no food at all unless we brought it. The large aid agencies simply could not get assistance down to street level fast enough to prevent widespread suffering.

Our fifty-acre center at Machava stayed mostly flooded. Fish were swimming in our church where we had such wonderful meetings in the Holy Spirit. The standing water was filled with snakes, bugs, algae and mosquitoes. Our schoolbooks and facilities were all ruined, along with all our mattresses. The boys' dorms were on higher ground, but we would have to rebuild for the girls. Wells, pumps, windmills and solar power systems needed complete repair.

We tested 100 of our neighbors in the Machava community, and 95 of them had malaria. After that we stopped testing and just handed out chloroquine to everyone. Our own daughter, Crystalyn, got malaria, along with 50 other children at our Zimpeto center.

Morale was high in the camps when the Gospel was preached and the love of God shown. Everyone was extremely receptive and grateful. We wanted to be poured out completely so that Jesus could do anything and everything He wished through us all. We never thought we would see such disaster, but against that backdrop we wanted the Holy Spirit to arrive and do more than we ever imagined. We knew that we might see a turn to God that could not come about any other way, and that God often did His best work in the worst situations. We wanted the people of Mozambique to find in Him the love they had always wanted but had never understood before. How wonderful it was to bring the weakest and loneliest we could find into the warm shelter of His heart, where there is complete safety.

Need and joy in the camps

What happened to Mozambique, this country where we lived, worked and came to know so well, was almost unbelievable to us. A three-day rainstorm turned into a natural disaster that required the largest humanitarian aid mobilization that Africa had ever seen. Southern Mozambique was one huge flood plain draining the highlands of South Africa and Zimbabwe, and there was no escape for whole towns and villages, many still beyond the range of rescue helicopters.

Mothers struggling in neck-deep currents drowned their own babies in their back slings. Stranded communities were reduced to eating the decayed flesh of dead cows, and children even roasted rats. Upper-story roofs in Xai-Xai collapsed under the weight of so many desperate survivors. Sewage and animal carcasses raised a terrible stench in the streets. Severe malnutrition set in among young children. Clean water was nearly impossible to find, even for rescue crews. Refugees were seen urinating in and drinking out of the same pools of water. Malaria victims lay motionless in the dirt with high fevers. Twenty-six camps with almost no facilities or provisions tried to care for 250,000 people.

Finally aid poured into Maputo's tiny airport, creating a logistical nightmare. Air traffic controllers were flown in from England to handle the load. After weeks of delay, the government expedited customs, but still the fine details of every shipment took hours and days for officials to write out without computers. Organizing and delivering goods to the camps, and then by air to still-stranded populations, overtaxed the capabilities of the world's largest disaster relief organizations. And still the cry was, "Too little, too late." There weren't enough helicopters in all of Africa to handle the need.

We assumed responsibility for a second camp of three thousand flood victims, this one north of Maputo near the severe floodwaters. To get there we had to wade through water waist-deep or deeper for an hour, take surface transport at exorbitant cost (fuel had to be carried in on heads), wade for another hour, take another "capa" ride and then wade again. Heidi kept falling into holes and mud, arriving totally drenched. Helicopters brought in survivors all through the day and landed them in three main areas south of Xai-Xai.

In the camps we found huge joy as thousands listened to the Gospel and devoured tracts even before they ate the bread we brought. These flood victims, many weak and sick, and all without possessions, loved to sit and learn about our Lord Jesus. They responded, they worshiped, they prayed and wept in repentance for themselves and the sins of their nation. They sang and danced. They were thrilled when we sent ministry teams. They needed more than pallets of beans and rice. As the president's secretary-general told us, his people needed love. They needed comfort and warmth. They needed to be hugged. They needed assurance and faith. They needed the Lord and all that is in His heart.

Mozambique was still a land of paganism, witchcraft and ancestor worship for many. The head of the Renamo, the political party that narrowly lost a recent national election, declared that this disaster was the work of angry "spirits" taking revenge over a miscount of the votes. Syncretism, illiteracy and rural isolation were other obstacles to hearing the clear Gospel. But in these camps people gathered together from their far-flung villages, eager and willing to listen to preaching and to receive ministry in the Holy Spirit. We asked Jesus to reign over this national calamity as only He could.

Facing the future in Mozambique

In a short time Mozambique went off the evening news around the world, but its pain increased as the consequences of the flooding took effect. This was one of the worst disasters relief agencies had ever seen. "We are shocked and can't believe the magnitude of the destruction and suffering we are seeing. It is daunting," said Brian Jones of the British International Rescue Dogs (BIRD).

Cyclones were not unusual during the rainy season in this part of the world, but to have three of them in quick succession was a once-in-a-lifetime occurrence. The many dams that should have controlled the flooding needed five times their reservoir capacity to be effective. Most years were quite dry, and Mozambique's rivers served to sustain life. But with this much rain, the rivers overran their banks and moved across the countryside in six-foot waves, destroying crops, tearing up roads and putting whole towns under water.

The floodwaters were beginning to go down, but heavy rains came back, halting relief efforts. Our own children's center at Machava had to be evacuated again, since some of our older children had gone back to begin cleaning up in spite of remaining water. Relief workers in the refugee camps were often themselves stranded and suffering without food and clean water. Large amounts of medical supplies were airlifted to Maputo, but because of bureaucracy and corruption much did not reach the field where it was most needed. Tens of thousands of victims who were exposed to contaminated water and the elements for weeks should have been vaccinated, but the necessary supplies and equipment were not available. Doctors and nurses working in the most desperate camps were expected to carry on with little or nothing. All over the camps children were contracting severe eye infections from insects breeding in the water, yet antibiotic eye ointments were scarce. Without cooking fuel, the people tried to eat raw corn maize and got sick. Some aid workers were even sent home for their own mental well-being, in spite of the need, so great was their stress.

Eventually we were feeding and trying to take care of some twelve thousand people in various camps, both in Maputo and north near the Limpopo River flooding. Support came in from friends, churches and agencies around the world, and volunteers arrived by land and air. We linked up with many other Christian groups, such as the Nazarene Church, Operation Mobilization, AirServ and churches in South Africa. We brought in containers for storage and set up logistical headquarters. We bought trucks for distribution. South African businessmen coordinated shipments of food, medicine and clothes to us. Yet the need still towered above our capacity, pointing us in the only direction we could move: more faith in Jesus!

Heidi and John Colby, a doctor from Hopkinsville, Kentucky, flew to Chibuto by helicopter to look for flood orphans and bring them back to our center. Chibuto is the airfield nearest the worst flooding of the Limpopo River, and air rescue teams had been bringing survivors there for weeks. Soon after Heidi's arrival, another cyclone passed by, and for three days she was stranded in the rain along with everyone else in her camp, as all aircraft were grounded.

And so she began to minister to the weak, sick, starving people huddling under tarps and other bits of shelter. She began in their own local tribal dialect, Changaan, and they immediately perked up with smiles. Heidi preached her heart out, and two thousand people came to Jesus. Soon the camp was singing and dancing—and many sobbed on their faces for their sins and the sins of the nation. They were starved for God. They went right past what food they had to receive prayer. As in other camps, they were overjoyed when Christians came to them with the only truly good news there is: the Gospel. They longed for Bibles and tracts and for worship meetings all through the day. Many camps had no Christian witness at all, and with such a prevalence of witchcraft and ancestor worship, the darkness was very great. This flood brought a poverty of spirit among the people that opened the way for Jesus when they heard about Him. They knew how much they needed

Him, and they were in position to become richer toward God than even the most comfortable Westerners.

Finally, on the third day, we were able to send a plane in to get Heidi, but it was a miracle. The runway was so muddy that only one other plane tried to land, and it broke its landing gear. Two hundred people were trying to get out on this one small planc, but the pilot took off with Heidi and John, and they got back safely with intense accounts of conditions at the camp.

Never in all our years in mission work had we ever imagined such ministry opportunity—such a chance to live out the commands of Jesus and demonstrate to the world that not even such calamity can separate us from the love of God. It was a huge joy to see Jesus come to these people and make them glad as only He could, even as they sat in the rain, completely destitute apart from Him.

A day in the bush with flood victims

By the end of March 2000, hundreds of thousands of Mozambicans were still left without homes and crops, and their misery would continue long after the world forgot them. We and our medical staff regularly flew helicopters at United Nations expense to visit the most remote and needy concentrations of flood victims we could find. On one of these missions Heidi and I flew with Dr. John Colby, Dr. Tony Dale, a friend from my missionary boarding school days, and his nurse Kathy Hanna.

The rivers had gone down some, but the flood plains were still marshy and impassable, stretching for hundreds of miles. The skies were filled with spectacular clouds in between the still-frequent rainstorms. Rainbows accented the Creator's artistry with pure, exquisite color. Brilliant light broke through from patches of deepest blue sky to shimmer on oceans of water and sparkle off the wakes of ducks and native boats. We appeared to be flying over natural wetlands, and all seemed well until we noticed the tops of trees and huts barely breaking the surface of the water. We skimmed the terrain at 150 feet as our local guide pointed our pilot this way and that trying to locate a village center on high ground where flood victims had congregated. We found the center and settled down through the trees in a blast of rotor wash that had children scampering away in fright. Our pilot noted the GPS coordinates so that we could be found at the end of the day.

Here was a community of people that probably had not had medical attention in their entire lives. The children had never seen white people and didn't know whether to be scared or curious. We introduced ourselves to the local leaders, who were profoundly grateful for our appearance. We decided to set up a "clinic" in a thatched round structure, opening our boxes of supplies on rough wooden benches. But first, Heidi led everyone in some worship songs in their local Changaan dialect, and that made them happy. Soon she was on her knees, worshiping the Lord over the flood, and the people followed, their hearts so hungry for a touch from Him.

Treatment began, and nearly everyone lined up with illnesses and complaints. They crowded and waited anxiously in the hot sun on the dirt. I went up and down the lines, trying to spot the worst cases, especially among children, and I began to find them. Babies in their mothers' slings were dripping with perspiration from malaria fever. Eyes were swollen and oozing with infections. Skin was covered with scabies. Old ladies were slumped over in pain and weakness. I counted out dosages of malaria medication into little bags while Kathy dispensed everything else as fast as she could. The doctors swabbed raw sores with antiseptic solution and listened to diseased hearts and lungs. Ear infections, venereal disease and arthritis kept cropping up. Antibiotics were squeezed by syringe into the mouths of crying, kicking babies. We laid hands on many, praying for God's merciful, healing touch. Those who could read got a Bible in their language and were overjoyed. It became clear that we were dealing with not just the aftermath of a flood, but a level of lifelong poverty incomprehensible in the West. These village folk might never see a doctor again.

We talked to them about their predicament. Their crops were all under water, and they had lost all they had. They needed seed as soon as the fields could be planted again, and basic farming tools. They didn't know how they would eat until then. Fruit and vegetables were nonexistent. We gave them as many vitamin tablets as we could.

A Swiss missionary had worked here, it turned out, and many had heard the basics of the Gospel, but witchcraft and syncretism conspired constantly to confuse many. I learned that the centers of some of the worst flooding, Chokwe and Chibuto, had an unusually high concentration of witch doctors. Now, however, almost everyone wanted to hear from the living God. They wanted the Truth, nothing less. They begged for church, for preaching, for Bibles and for prayer. "When are you coming back? Please come back! Please pray for us!" they cried in camp after camp. The floods concentrated many thousands of usually isolated peasants into centers where they thronged past stacks of relief maize, flour and sugar to get their hands on tracts.

We had to leave our village by five o'clock to make it back to Maputo by dark. We packed up early to leave time to sing and preach. We heard our returning chopper in the distance and began making our way out to the clearing where it would land. Heidi had her powered megaphone in hand, and the whole center fell in behind us singing and dancing, their African melodies and harmony floating out through the trees and over the watery fields up to the listening ears of Jesus Himself. We came unknown and unannounced, but in one day left as close family. The helicopter landed, the pilot surprised to see a whole congregation gathered around his flying machine. The people had heard a message, intense and full of glory, hope and victory. They prayed, hands folded and tears flowing. Everyone jumped and waved as we climbed in. The sun lowered in the sky, casting its warm, late glow over the greenery and the brown, glowing faces of a people touched by goodness. They were glad. They had seen and felt the love of God. And we had to go, disappearing mysteriously back toward lands beyond the river.

We flew, cotton in our ears for the noise, each with our own thoughts and prayers. We moved over islands, lakes and swamps, hardly able to make out the boundaries of a river out of control. Finally we came to the sea and skimmed many miles of untouched sand dunes painted by the sunset and splashed gently by waves of soft foam. In the far distance ahead of us was the silhouette on a hill that marked Maputo. On our way as we neared the city we circled around Chihango, our first children's center, now a watery bog filled with dangerous mosquitoes. We landed at Maputo International Airport, with its simple, little terminal sitting among lines of helicopters and transport planes flown in from around to world to deal with this catastrophe. It looked like such a big operation, but it barely touched countless population centers like the one we just visited, and there were many that had not been reached yet. Just two days earlier John and Tony visited an island in the Limpopo River with ten thousand survivors of the flood who had just been found after more than a month of isolation and exposure.

Jesus was jealous of *everything*. He was washing Mozambique clean—of idolatry, witchcraft, corruption, indifference, stealing, violence—everything. The people in the camps knew as never before that Jesus was their only hope. The Lord wanted that rarest of human emotions, *love for Him*, to sweep over a land bereft of all else.

We continued to add children to our huge family at our Zimpeto center. They were up at dawn each day to sing and pray. One Thursday night they gathered under our tent for ministry, kneeling in the dirt by the dim light of a few bulbs, caring nothing for the muggy, soggy conditions as they worshiped the King. We asked, "Who wants to be His servant and go out to call the poor to His wedding feast?" Many responded, weeping on their faces in the mud up front where we have our altar calls. The next Saturday three truckloads of them joined us and our pastors at the cashew factory to help preach and pray for the refugees. We sent "the least of these" to camps everywhere, and they were part of God's answer in that critical hour.

We were still in camps every day, buying and distributing many thousands of bread loaves and ministering with all our strength. As we preached we gave out Bibles, and such was the demand that we gave Bibles only to those who wanted to become preachers and be used by God to save Mozambique from all its sin and misery.

A flight to Zongoene

The wind was whipping up at Maputo International Airport as Heidi and I packed our Cessna 206 with blankets and clothes. The sky to the north, where we wanted to fly, was getting dark. A fuel truck had just topped off our tanks, but soon we were huddling under the wings in pouring rain, wondering if we would go anywhere that day. But the squall soon passed, the sun burst out and after entering GPS coordinates for Zongoene we were off.

The day was spectacular. We headed up the coast to the northeast at 3,500 feet, dodging a few brilliant, white clouds that accented the rich, deep blue of sky and sea. A direct route would have taken us 7 miles offshore, so to enjoy the view we followed 85 miles of white, completely unspoiled sand dunes along the beach to get to our destination, the mouth of the flooded Limpopo River. All along the way, just inland across the sand dunes, we could see an awesome plain of devastation. Prime farmland as far as the eye could see was under muddy, brown water. Zongoene was a community of thousands that had been isolated by floodwaters for weeks without help and had not even appeared in government statistics. Friends maintain a lodge on the beach in this area, and after circling around several times to inspect the situation, we landed on their grass airstrip, now barely higher than the swampy bogs that surrounded it. Just a week earlier the runway had been another watery inlet of the Limpopo.

Villagers came running up to the plane, beaming, so glad to see someone from the outside world. It took a while, but eventually the lodge staff appeared on their four-wheel-drive buggies after a struggle through deep mud. And sure enough, Dr. Tony Dale and his nurse Kathy, our medical staff that we had sent to Zongoene three days before by helicopter, showed up, too—grubby, cheery and experienced off-roaders by now. The lodge had a four-wheel-drive truck, but a driveshaft U-joint was broken, and we were left with front-wheel-drive—not good in these conditions. But we climbed in anyway with everything we brought and began charging through water and up soggy banks the best we could, stopping to dig out again and again. We made progress and headed for the nearby villages, picking up the community chief, and his guard armed with an AK-47, along the way.

Now we were part of a most improbable scene. We circled the whole area with our ex-communist chief in the back of our pickup, shouting out invitations to our church meeting through Heidi's powered megaphone! And then the people came—appearing out of bushes and across their cleanly-swept dirt courtyards from their thatched huts until hundreds were following us, some actually running right behind us for miles. Laughing and jumping with excitement, they all converged on the church: a big, long, plain, bare, cement block building that our Christian friends at the lodge built as a mission outreach.

Everyone jammed the church. It was late in the afternoon and getting dark. There were no lights, of course. The crowd was delighted that Heidi spoke Changaan, the local dialect. Her megaphone was distorted, running out of battery power, but she preached herself hoarse anyway. They all wanted to hear everything they could of the Gospel. They were so eager, responding and crying out to God. Hands went up all over the dim interior as young and old declared their faith and desire.

Then we distributed our blankets and clothes. The village's armed guard was struggling to keep order. The cold season was approaching in Mozambique, and a blanket was a priceless treasure. In their desperation, mothers climbed over each other to reach our pile. The guard did his best, but still hands reached through bodies and snatched what was left, and girls ran off squealing with joy. The disorder didn't get dangerous, and even the guard had a grin on his face, so great was it to see such help made available. The clothes were distributed next, and again extreme poverty produced a frenzy of desperation and excitement until every scrap of cloth was grabbed.

We hadn't planned to stay so late, but we couldn't stop what we were doing. We finally made it back to the airstrip after dark. It was a black, moonless night. The stars were so clear way out there. The surf crashed only a hundred yards away. But I couldn't make out the runway boundaries without help, so we positioned a truck at the far end with its headlights pointing at us. With five of us on board, our engine roaring, our beacon flashing and all our lights on, we bumped down the grass on our oversize tires toward the twin points of light in the distance. Airborne, we got an IFR clearance back to Maputo, and then it was a quiet, peaceful flight, the stars obscured only occasionally by patches of cloud. Ninety-five percent of Mozambican houses have no electricity, and there were no brightly-lit towns to follow on the way. We saw almost nothing until the approach lights of Maputo's airport showed in the far distance. We glided onto a huge concrete runway, back in relative civilization, though except for a tower voice the place seemed shut down, with no activity at all apart from us. It was a long taxi back to our hangar, and again we were all silent, reflecting on another day of service to the King in a land crying out to Him.

Floods, famine and harvest

One beautiful day late in April, I watched towering cumulus clouds to the west lined with rich orange and lavender in the setting sun, a climax to another lavish display of African splendor. The wildness, great distances, endless beaches and skies of grandeur had spoiled us. But now we were spoiled by more than God's hand of nature. He was bringing a nation to Himself, stripping away all competition and finally conquering hearts until He was the object of desire among thousands and thousands of destitute flood victims. The whole countryside was presenting itself for spiritual harvest. Everywhere we went, in camp after camp, the people begged for the things of God. "We can't even remember what we lost," they cried. "We just want the Word of God!" God used His own methods, and He was getting His desire. He loves to be loved, and the Mozambican people were bowing at His feet. We were spoiled by such a God, by such a Spirit, by such love and by the work He gave us to do.

It had been more than two months since Mozambique's disastrous flooding began. We were traveling, preaching, mobilizing, planning, driving, flying—stunned all the while by the harvest we saw before us. We could hardly get to our mail and accounting, so urgent and wonderful was the ministry on all sides. This terrible calamity that beggared the capabilities of the United Nations and the world's largest relief organizations brought a people to its knees.

The material situation

Official statistics showed that over eight thousand tons of food had been delivered, two-thirds by air. One hundred twenty-one accommodation centers were set up, and more were added every day. Ministries, committees, working groups, donors and officials were surveying, collaborating, integrating and coordinating. Every few days we pored over situation reports concerning food, agriculture, health, water and sanitation, shelter and logistics. We and the people were so grateful for all this relief activity and cooperation between churches, relief agencies, the government and the military.

But God saw more deeply, and the actual situation was far more drastic than officially portrayed. To receive an intercessory spirit after the heart of God for Mozambique was shattering. We wanted more than to report simply that we were doing a good job. We wanted the truth—and the ability to feel what God feels.

The best efforts of all involved were not nearly enough to

deal with the suffering that directly resulted from the floods. Food—bags of cornmeal and little else—were dropped off in a certain number of concentrated centers, but there were so many people that rations were still pitiful. We had a ministry team that worked in the Chokwe camp, one of the most-supplied with over seventy thousand refugees in a massive sea of tents, and still we met groups who had not eaten at all in days. Maize shipments were delivered to warehouses near these central camps, but there was hardly any infrastructure to carry them farther into the many villages and islands of people on the periphery of these camps and beyond.

More and more aid workers were getting tired, losing motivation and going home. Funds for aviation fuel were running out. Few organizations were scheduling air transport flights anymore. There was only a handful of doctors to serve hundreds of thousands of flood victims. For weeks we had been flying our medical and ministry teams into completely unserved areas. The sick were walking ten and fifteen miles through water to get to our clinics. At one point the UN World Food Program and Doctors Without Borders asked Iris Ministries to go into six more areas where thousands of people had been left desperate without aid since the floods began.

Many families were separated by the floods and the rescue operations. In one province it was reported that thirty to forty percent of the children could not find their parents. Without telephones and community records, and with their huts and other recognizable landmarks washed away, thousands of children were lost and wandering. We may never have an idea of how many people were drowned and swept away by strong currents.

We got reports from our more than three hundred churches spread throughout the north, far beyond the major camps that received most of the available international aid. Communication was very difficult, but eventually we were able to make phone connections and learned that these churches had also met with devastation.

Although the government reported that one million people

were displaced from their homes by the flood, many more millions lost their crops. The fierce wind and rain from the cyclones in the north tore up the fields, even on high ground, leaving incredible numbers of people without food or aid. Nearly all our pastors were by necessity subsistence farmers, and they had to work their fields to feed themselves. Now even that source of food was gone.

Some pastors at our Bible school in Maputo heard that their wives and children were seen walking long distances to search for food. Other families just disappeared without word. We had leading pastors with no home to return to at all. Pastors still in the north were finding shelter in what was left of their church buildings, huddling on cement or dirt floors and shifting around to stay out of rain. Walls were blown down and roofs torn off. Most in these areas were hungry and without medical care.

God's answer

For a year in our Bible school and meetings we had been pouring everything we could spiritually into our pastors and older children. Now they were being used to bring in the harvest. Every day we sent them into the refugee camps by truck, helicopter, plane or boat—however we could. Identified by our Iris caps and shirts as officially registered aid workers, they were given freedom by the government to pray and minister everywhere they went.

Our pastors had endured Mozambique's civil war and knew from experience the difference between satanic cruelty and the love of God. Many had endured hardship for years to be soldiers of Jesus Christ. They were all thrilled to be in the King's service. They didn't seem to get tired, and they prayed for everyone. Refugees begged them to return—with more Bibles and more teaching. As they preached demons manifested themselves, and the pastors cast them out. The word spread quickly: This Jesus has power! Many heard the name of Jesus for the first time. Others had known only cults and various syncretistic, perverted versions of Christianity, but they were now receiving the pure milk of the Word.

After two months of national trauma, the Gospel was spreading almost unhindered around us. Local pastors in Maputo came to us, wanting to join our ministry and relief efforts. From government officials down to the smallest street children, hearts were open to Jesus on a scale we had never seen before. In the dumps, on the streets, in the refugee camps, in remote villages, among the poor and starving, a nation wanted to know Jesus. Yes, the people needed aid, they needed food and clothes, but now they also knew how much they needed Jesus. We cried to Him that He would supply us with all that we needed to bring in the harvest—all the wisdom, energy, stamina, resources, faith, power and workers we needed to please Him and finish what He set before us to do.

North to the Zambezi—May 2000

Rain pounded us all night on the coast at Beira, five hundred miles north of our center in Maputo. At dawn dark clouds were turning and boiling overhead as they swept inland, driven by gusting wind. Whitecaps marked crashing breakers far out to sea. Another cyclone was bearing down on Mozambique, we would learn later, but we wanted to get north another hundred miles that morning by plane. Our pastors had brought us reports of catastrophic crop damage from storms and flooding all along the main rivers where we had hundreds of churches. With roads washed out and no telephone communication, we wanted to see for ourselves the conditions in the Zambezi River area, far beyond any previous relief efforts.

Out over the African bush to the northern horizon we could see heavy streaks of rain angling down from blackening build-ups, but their tops were not high and soon our Cessna was climbing and banking toward the shadowy mists. With me were Gordon and Tanneken, from our base in Maputo, and Pastor Amori, our guide, who also helps us oversee the churches of that vast province. We skimmed the hills and trees at five hundred feet, ducking even lower to keep clear of stormy gray patches reaching toward the ground. Rain pelted our windshield, and cool drops blew against our faces from the air vents. Below us pristine wilderness slid by at 150 miles an hour, marked only occasionally by thatched huts in well-swept clearings. We were as far from the busy airways of civilization as we could get.

For an hour we rode the winds and currents of the storm, drinking in the panoramic drama of land and sky all around us and tasting up close the visual flavor of Africa. On and off turbulence reminded us of our unsettled, fluid path through the sky, taking us like birds where we could never go before.

The rains were very localized, and as the famous ribbon of the Zambezi materialized in the distance, we broke out into brilliant sunlight. Nothing stopped our vision. Mountains rose far beyond the river toward Malawi. The African savannah was before us in splendor, and down there along the plain in village after village were our people, thousands and thousands of our sheep, each longing for the Creator of all the world.

The Zambezi upon us, we turned and cruised the river, just above the water and sandbars, banking back and forth as we followed its turns. Pastor Amori was so excited. He had an amazing heart for evangelism, as did so many of our pastors, and he had been all over this Zambezi territory on foot, planting churches. He traveled incredible distances, tramping through the bush for many days and weeks, and then we gave him new, colorful preaching shoes—Nike cross-trainers.

Now, though, Amori was pointing out from our plane all the villages where we had churches. "There's one, and there's another one!" he would cry. "And there's the pastor's hut! And over there!" We overflew dirt airstrips: Mopeia, Caia, Chibougua, Goma—there are over one hundred charted bush strips in Mozambique, and we had churches near most of them. Eighty percent of Mozambique's people lived in these isolated rural areas, where white missionaries were almost never seen, and which were almost completely untouched by the traditional churches of the main towns.

But revival was blazing through the countryside. We had 350 churches by then, and expected 400 by October. Our pastors were on fire with zeal. They endured any hardship to carry the Word even farther. They could only be motivated by the supernatural love of God. They had raised at least five from the dead. They came streaming to our Bible school from all over the country. A group arrived from Beira by bus after wading through waist-deep mud and water for five miles at a break in the road to get on another bus to the next break. One pastor had club feet and another was almost crippled, but they struggled through anyway. These were the most destitute pastors we had yet received, wearing only rags, bringing nothing with them. They were leaving their families for months in order to learn the Word of God. No one had a Bible or a bicycle or even a toothbrush. We spent weeks locating them, sending out messengers on foot when necessary to deliver food and bus money.

We kept flying over the river, carefully studying the cultivated fields along the way. Every stand of maize was dead. The terrible floods and winds since February had taken out all the crops, even as far north as the Zambezi. The rivers had gone down, but the ground was muddy and swampy. The people had no seed for new crops, and the dry season had come. Belongings were washed away, and families all over southern Mozambique lacked even hoes to begin working their farms again. Two million land mines still in the ground made farming dangerous, especially since known minefields had been shifted by moving water.

We followed the Zambezi for another sixty miles, glorying in the beauty of the day, the unending variety of the magnificent river and in the grace of God for His mercy poured out in so many hearts even to the ends of the earth. Some of our mud-and-stick churches were built right near the river's banks; others were in clearings off in the bush. Many were storm-damaged. Almost all were without electricity or even pit latrines. We always had to bring generators with our sound systems when we came to preach.

Finally we arrived at Mutarara, a main town on the Zambezi with a bridge for road traffic north to Malawi. We had eight churches in this general area, but there was another airstrip across the river at Sena, where we had none. We banked sharply to follow our satellite coordinates to the strip, dropped quickly and found it just before us. The field was very narrow and rough. A goat saw us and ran for its life. Rocks, mounds and patches of weeds were in our path. We touched down smoothly enough, raced toward a hump in the runway and flew off it for a few more feet. We finally coasted to a stop and found ourselves surrounded by tall grass and hills, and a village. Everyone gathered around us, excited and curious. Pastor Amori knew the local dialect and could interpret. We gathered in a clearing, and soon we were preaching and having church. That's just what the villagers wanted. In minutes they were repenting and worshiping, their hands in the air and their hearts with the King. All wanted Jesus; all wanted a church in their village; all wanted us to send them a pastor. Only one could read, so we gave him a Bible with strict instructions to read to the others. They were glad and could hardly believe we had dropped in on them like this. And they waved and cried as we taxied back to takeoff position.

Heading back to Beira at high altitude and in clear air, we passed over a vast countryside. Still Pastor Amori knew every community. "Look there!" he pointed out. "People walk all day from 7 A.M. to 7 P.M. from that village to reach one of our churches because we don't have one in their village, and then they stay for three days of meetings and walk back! We have to start another church there!" Tanneken, Gordon and I began to understand. We could start a new church every day if we had the time and energy. The harvest was ready all over Mozambique.

After meeting with more pastors and planning upcoming conferences, we continued our flight to Maputo. Grand, cumulus clouds surrounded us with a heavenly wonderland. We broke in and out of them, dancing to more turbulence—and got our visual senses dazzled by fresh rainbows, flashing reflections off more rivers and lakes and the intense brilliance of cloud tops pierced by purest sunlight. We imagined the glories of heaven, the symphony of light, color and sound around the throne of God and the wonder of that love in His heart. How excellent it was to serve the King, to be His slave and to be one with Him in spirit.

The traditional Chinese dwelling and courtyard in Kunming, China, where the events of *Visions Beyond the Veil* took place

Boys in the heat of the Maputo city dump, covered with flies, and glad to hear about Jesus

House in the Maputo dump

Worship in the garbage dump

Gathering children for church in the dump

Our wedding, May 1980

Beatrice and Constancia

Valentino, emotionally healed after his mother was beaten to death by three bandits with him in her arms

Baptism at our Machava children's center

Helena and Beatrice

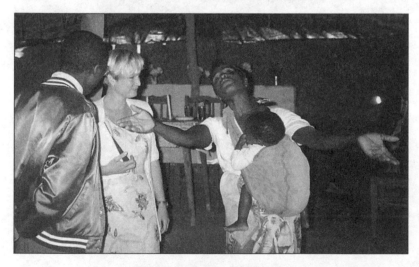

Rosa, back from the dead

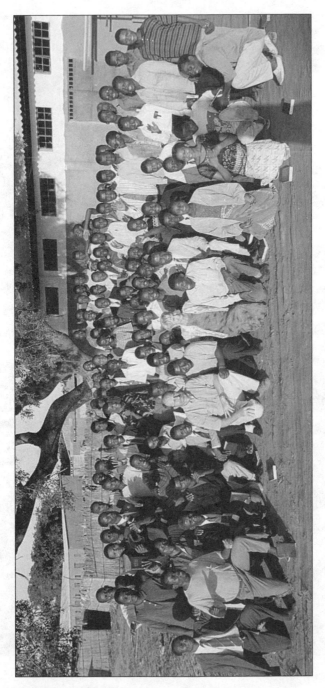

Bible college graduation, Zimpeto

Pastors Rego, Joni and Surpresa, who have all raised the dead in Jesus' name

Altar call with Pastor Rego

New beginnings at Machava

Surpresa Sithole, founder with us of Partners in Harvest/Iris Africa

Zimpeto family

With our family at Zimpeto

Revival in the bush

The Zambezi River in flood

Maize distribution in the flood

Our pastors' conference in Bangula, Malawi

Preaching in Marromeu

Conference cooking in the bush

Graduation and ordination

The Bread of Life for hungry flood victims

Resurrection life

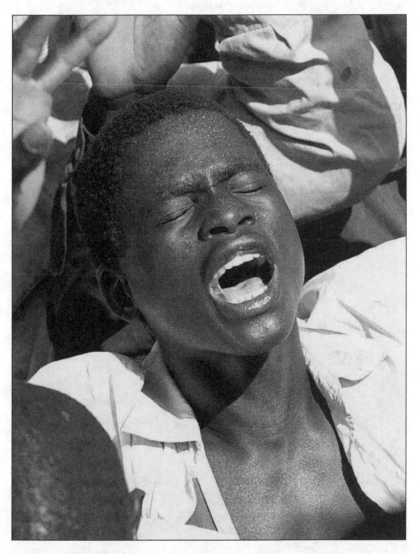

Adoration

Our children loving Jesus

The flying machine

The Baker family

Starting a new church right on the runway

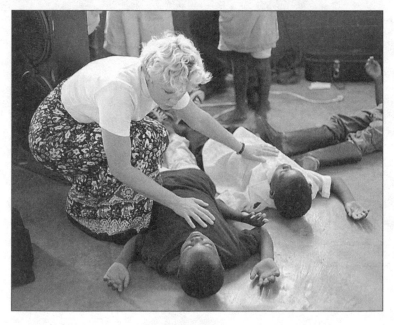

Ministry time

Waiting for bread in the flood

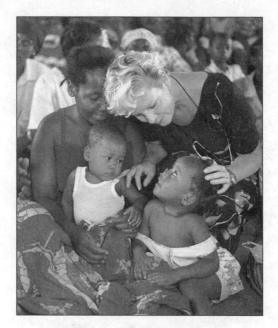

Ministry to flood victims

Receiving the Word with our family

Church planting

Heidi doing street ministry in Hong Kong

Floods in Maputo

Teaching pastors in the bush

Hallelujah!

Joy in a mud church

Wholehearted worship

Our boys in prayer

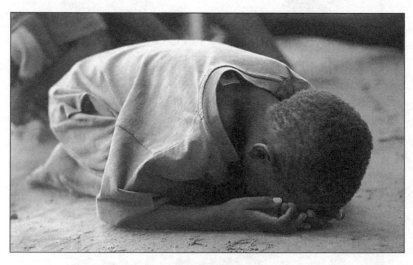

True humility

The road to our center after the flood

Refugees in the flood

Lost in worship

Shipping food relief in the flood

He is risen!

Chapter 7

Floods of Revival

Our corner of Africa opened up wide to the Gospel after the severe floods in Mozambique of early 2000. Worldwide attention was focused on a nation that previously had endured decades of war, drought and economic disaster in almost complete obscurity. The flooding was savage, but Mozambicans learned their need for God. Christians around the world interceded for the nation and gave generously with open hearts and hands. Whole rural populations came together in refugee camps and heard the Gospel all at once. Tens of thousands came to Jesus in our meetings, and other missions saw rich fruit as well.

Our red-hot, Spirit-filled bush pastors, trained in our short-term Bible school, dived into the camps and ministered with energy from God Himself. As the numbers of believers climbed, we planted new churches, appointed new pastors and brought them to Bible school, too. Spiritual fervor among the flood victims shot up. They found out Jesus could drive out demons, heal the sick and replace witch doctors with grace, beauty and love. They wanted Bibles more than rice and blankets, more than anything. We'd arrive, and they'd cry, "Let's have church!"

As the floodwaters receded, the refugee camps dispersed. The homeless tried to start over, many in new locations. But our churches remained intact as pastors stayed with their people and they continued to seek God together. As fast as pastors came through our Bible school, more rose up until we had almost a hundred in our three-month session. We also found that our pastors and network of more than four hundred churches in remote rural areas provided us with the best possible distribution system for relief goods among those who needed help the most.

With our churches multiplying so quickly and our Bible school doubling in size in a year, there was a huge hunger for the things of God among us. One way of satisfying that hunger was to hold our unique style of "bush conferences" in central locations for as many pastors and church people as we could get together. Our donated Cessna 206 aircraft gave us and our visiting speakers the terrific ability to travel long distances frequently and on tight schedules, regardless of road conditions.

Fire in Malawi—September 2000

Malawi stretched ahead, its hills rising seven thousand feet below us from the Zambezi River valley of Mozambique. Pure, dazzling cumulus clouds added grandeur to the fresh, clear air of the north, far from the smoky brush fires that polluted the skies of Maputo around our center in the south. Heidi and I were squeezed into our Cessna light plane, sharing precious space with everything we needed for a crusade in the bush: sound system, generator, tents, sleeping bags, lights, tools, lots of water. With worship music playing in our headsets, we prepared our hearts.

We were excited, studying the huts passing below us and praying to understand the needs of yet another country and mission field. A peak ahead blocked normal radio transmission to Blantyre, so we used shortwave to reach Lilongwe and explain our intentions. What were we doing in Malawi, they wanted to know. We were holding a conference for almost one hundred of our churches in the unlikely town of Bangula in Malawi's southern tip, and we needed to be there that night.

I (Rolland) had last visited Malawi in May, when we had eighteen churches that resulted from a two-day visit by our staff a year earlier. Now we had more than a hundred churches in this dusty, forgotten corner of the country where white missionaries were almost never seen. Thousands of believers had begged for this conference. They could hardly believe we were coming this far to be with them, and they were so excited. Many were walking for days from their villages to our meetings. Even our leading pastors from Mozambique were enduring long, tortuous bus journeys over terrible roads to help us with this wildfire revival.

Fueled up at Blantyre, we headed for Bangula, still sixty miles away. I knew it only by its GPS coordinates. We dropped over the hills down to a low plain, hot and shimmering in haze. I picked out rivers and landmarks I recognized from my chart. I hardly knew what to expect. Silva, our lead pastor in Malawi, had been working for months getting the word out about these meetings. Was anyone coming? How would we take care of them?

Up came a river that I knew ran right by Bangula. A town materialized, but it was small and spread out. I saw dirt roads and dry brush, but no runway where the map said it should be. I circled around. "Help me look, Heidi," I asked. "I don't see any kind of airport!" But there was a curious open field at the center of town, crisscrossed by footpaths. That couldn't be the airfield. There were cows all over it and people wandering everywhere. Then I saw the letters B-A-N-G-U-L-A dug in the dirt, obviously to be seen from the air, and a few markers at the corners of the field. A truck charged across the field, bouncing over the ruts through the crowds, and I recognized it as one of ours, driven up days earlier from Mozambique. I skimmed the ground to inspect the surface. There were holes, ditches and anthills, rocks and bushes, but I picked out a relatively safe line. Tanneken Fros, on our staff from Israel, was in the truck and waving energetically as we flew by her. This was the place. Thousands of children were streaming across the field to watch us land. A few older guys frantically waved them, and the cows, to the side with sticks. I flew around the pattern for another approach and coasted in with full flaps, settling down as easily as possible on our oversize tires. The ground was rough and our plane shook and vibrated to a stop in a cloud of dust. We were down and safe—and inundated with jumping, excited kids.

It was obvious that a plane hadn't landed here in years. This was an event! Everyone was staring. What did we bring? What was in that plane? We dragged out our big speakers and heavy generator and were mobbed by helpers. Somehow everything got loaded into the truck, we found guards for the plane and we were off to our first meeting.

It wasn't in a church, or even a building. One of our Christians had a field with a couple of mud huts. We got there by driving in and out of deep gullies along a dry riverbed, trying to remember how to get back. There wasn't much left of the town. Clearly the economy was dead. The countryside was gripped by drought. Dust blew down the street in swirls. People sat in the shade and stared without energy. The few shops were almost bare. All was in disrepair. But we found our "conference," a big band of ragged, dirt-poor, country peasants who had been waiting for us all day. Tanneken had bought them sticks and plastic tarps, which they had put up between the huts for shelter. They had even nailed together some rough boards for a speaker's platform, with its own roof of tarp.

It was windy, the tarps were flapping and dust was blowing everywhere. A couple thousand people were trying to find bits of shade. We set up the generator way off in the bushes where it wouldn't be heard, positioned our big speakers and hooked up our heavy amp, and we had a sound system! What a rarity.

This gathering was the poorest we had seen yet in Africa. All came without food. None of the children had shoes. Obviously, most had never received medical care. There were swollen, infected eyes and feet and terrible scabs and sores everywhere. To feed them we bought big cooking pots and all the beans and maize available in town. Our ladies stirred these pots over wood fires through the day, babies strapped to their backs. They carried water on their heads from a well in a nearby village. We bought straw mats for everyone to lie on at night, and they slept with their colorful skirts wrapped tightly around them. There were no lights apart from the flashlights we brought. We dug our own pit latrines.

But we came to preach, and we poured our hearts out for three days. Is everyone hungry for Jesus? Do we want His presence and touch? Do we want to be filled with the Holy Spirit? Do we want to repent of all our evil and idolatry? Yes, yes, yes, yes! What have we come here for? Nothing less than the love of God in Christ Jesus, who died for us! We'll never get love from a witch doctor. We'll never find enough in our families. We'll only find it in Jesus. If we have Him, we'll have everything!

We taught all we could from the Word of God in our short time together. The people flooded forward in every meeting, kneeling in the dust and hot sun during the day and in the dark at night. They wanted everything they could get. There was no resistance to the Gospel. They knew they were poor and helpless. This was their last chance, their only hope.

Their response grew, and then on the last day the floodgates of heaven were opened. Heidi preached from the book of James on the practical realities of holiness, trying to condense a training program for pastors into one session. New churches were forming almost every day, and we had to teach leaders quickly what they most needed to know. Did they want the purity of God? Did they want to be washed by the blood? Did they want the power of the Holy Spirit? Did they want the wisdom of God to lead their people?

We prayed for just the pastors first. They threw themselves down before God, oblivious of heat, wind and blowing dirt. A mighty cry of prayer went up to heaven. Young and old wept together. Rivers of tears flowed. Hands reached toward God. Many were shaking in their intensity, unaware of anyone else but Him. Lost in worship and desire, many poured their hearts out in tongues. We invited everyone to jump into the things of God, to come forward, join the pastors and seek Him. And then for hours our conference became something like a Day of Pentecost for Malawi. No one cared about time, appearance or comfort. Even children were hit with the fire of God. Waves of glory and gratitude rolled over us all. The roar of prayer continued. Jesus was getting what He wanted: extreme passion for Him!

This was what we came for, an outpouring of the Holy Spirit: visions, miracles, utter repentance and the richest love in the universe crashing down like a mighty, pounding cataract on the poor and abandoned of the world. May the fresh, cool, refreshing mist of this living waterfall be felt all over Africa and the world. May the brilliance of its perfection spread everywhere with thundering power. May the Holy Spirit roll like a tidal wave over the hopelessness of this entire continent, undoing Satan's worst.

A dangerous cholera outbreak

Two months into 2001 the rivers of central Mozambique continued to rise, cutting many thousands of our own church members off from food supplies and medical help. Upstream dams were being opened up to prevent them from overflowing and breaking. The rains continued, and now again Mozambique's government was helpless without international assistance.

Challenges to our faith in Jesus did not stop. Even as we received daily reports of desperation from the flooded north, a terrible outbreak of cholera hit our center at Zimpeto near the capital city of Maputo. We now think the cholera was introduced by contaminated food brought into a wedding in our church. The disease is wildly contagious, and within days we had taken seventy children, pastors and workers to a special cholera hospital in town. This was actually a big tent, strictly quarantined, filled with "cholera tables," bare wood beds with holes in them and buckets underneath for nonstop diarrhea and vomiting. Every patient was on an IV drip.

Many had died in this emergency hospital. Maputo's health

officials were terrified of a city-wide epidemic. Maputo's director of health put her finger in Heidi's face and told her, "You will be responsible for killing half of Maputo!" Everyday health officials came to our center, desperately trying to identify the source of the cholera and contain its spread. Soon the city police were involved, intent on shutting down our entire center and ministry. For days nothing seemed to help. We were washing and disinfecting everything. Our trucks were making hospital runs day and night. Our own clinic was filled with children on IVs. Our staff was completely exhausted.

Only Heidi was allowed to visit the tent hospital. Every day she would go in and spend hours and hours with our kids, holding them, soaking them in prayer, declaring that they would live and not die. They vomited on her, covered her with filth and slowly grew weaker. Many were on the edge of death, their eyes sunken and rolling back. The doctors were shocked by her lack of concern for herself and were certain she would die along with many of our children.

Our stress level was the highest ever. We remembered how we had been evicted from our first center in early 1997, and we just couldn't take that again. We had been preaching salvation and deliverance with all our hearts to these children we had rescued out of the streets and dump, and now they were slipping away right in front of us. Twenty of our pastors from the north were also in the tent and dying. Some of our weaker pastors desperately wanted to go home, certain that they would all die if they stayed with us. Heidi and I were ready yet again to quit if God did not do something.

But during all of this the Holy Spirit kept falling on our meetings. Again and again all visitors would come to Jesus and hungrily drink in His presence. A strong spirit of intercession came over our stronger pastors, who would pray all hours, not only for our cholera victims, but for the suffering of the whole nation. Intercessory prayer groups in the U.S. and Canada and around the world began to pray intensely for us.

Our entire future in Mozambique was in question. No one had any more answers. Our weakness was complete. Then some of our children began coming home from the hospital, even as others were being taken there. And then there were no more new cases. Extraordinary. And then everyone was home! Just like that, the cholera was gone, and Heidi was fine.

The doctors and nurses at the hospital were in a state of shock and wonder. The director of health again put a finger in Heidi's face: "You! This is God! The only reason you got through this was God! You and dozens of these children should be dead!" Eight of the medical staff there wanted to work with us immediately. "This is miraculous! You know God! We've never seen God do anything like this. We've never seen such love! We don't want to work here anymore. We want to work with you!"

Several visitors to our center who came down with cholera did die after returning to their huts and refusing to go to the hospital. And we heard that one of our pastors had died, but that report turned out to be mistaken. We did not lose a single person who lived with us at Zimpeto.

So in a matter of days our worst crisis ever turned into a wave of peace and joy at our center. We worshiped until all hours, beholding His beauty in our hearts and enjoying His company. Our pastors and children were laughing and filled with excitement. What about the flooding up north? What about the thousands who were sick and hadn't eaten in weeks? We didn't know exactly what Jesus was going to do through us yet, but our faith had grown to new heights. May we trust Him always and see Him glorified with our own eyes as we walk with Him even in the valley of the shadow of death. May you be encouraged, too, as you read this, and join us in serving the King!

Jesus is in Marromeu!—March 2001

The rain was pouring down, and it was pitch dark. Mud and water were all around. Clouds of mosquitoes were biting. The air was steamy hot. Heidi and I were tightly packed on a little cement platform under a tin roof along with hundreds of villagers. Our sound system was turned up high, and our generator labored under the load. We were preaching our hearts out. There were ten thousand people out there listening to us, not moving in their wet, barefoot, ragged misery. They had been streaming in all day from every direction, wading through chest-deep floodwater for hours to get to our meeting in Marromeu's central square. Somehow the word got out about our first meeting that morning, when Jesus began spontaneously healing people across the listening crowd. The cry spread across the fields and floodwaters, on foot and by canoe—"Jesus is in Marromeu!" They came to find Him, and kept coming until more people were gathered in Marromeu than the little town had ever seen, even when the president of Mozambique visited.

They hadn't come for food. We were only able to bring two 45-kilogram bags of beans in our Cessna. The shops were bare, as the few supply roads were under water. Thousands had lost everything in the flood and hadn't eaten in days or weeks. Many couldn't find the rest of their families. But everyone here understood one thing: They needed Jesus! Everyone responded for prayer; everyone wanted Him, His forgiveness, His life, His salvation. No one had any answers apart from Him. We prayed with them into the night. Jesus completely healed a lady who had gone totally blind and deaf—her husband had left her because she was no good anymore. She and her family were so thrilled they didn't know what to do. That testimony went out, and for the next three days people kept coming to Marromeu to find Jesus.

For months the entire Zambezi River plain had been flooded, all the way from the higher west side of central Mozambique to the ocean on the east. The waters were not recognizable as a river anymore. As far as the eye could see from our low-flying Cessna, huts and fields were covered. Only rooftops and trees here and there extended above the swirling, muddy currents. This was vast, primitive bush country, far more inaccessible than the southern floods of the previous year. Towns were linked by a few narrow, rough dirt roads, hard and slow to negotiate even in dry seasons. During rain they become unusable. And for the second rainy season in a row, Mozambique experienced record-breaking, torrential rain. Yet again, international aid was necessary to keep hundreds of thousands of people alive.

Helicopters pulled families out of the water. Whole communities were forced to move into government refugee camps indefinitely. These camps were on hilly higher ground, and we flew into those with usable airstrips. Marromeu is the last major town on the Zambezi before the great river reaches the Indian Ocean, but it was too isolated by the flood to receive any relief agency food. Its grassy runway was too wet and soft for large transport aircraft, and the few available cargo helicopters, which were incredibly expensive to operate, could not carry nearly enough for all its people each day. Commodities piled up in government food depots, brought by the UN World Food Program and other agencies, but the infrastructure needed to get food to where it was most needed among the people was lacking.

For three days we met with our more than twenty pastors from the Marromeu area. Their grass and mud churches were under water. They were huddling in town, trying to survive, crying out to God for help. Their people were all desperate for food. They were thrilled by our arrival and moved to tears by our small supply of beans, brought just for them. "Jesus has not forgotten us!" they wept. Loudly they called on God for mercy and grace. They were ecstatic about the miracles of healing. Everyone was encouraged, thrilled and grateful.

We connected with Jesus Alive Ministries (JAM), which produced milled maize with health additives at their plant farther south, and agreed to have our pastors help distribute their food. They landed once at Marromeu, but their heavy turboprop aircraft had to be towed out of soft ground by a tractor from a nearby sugar mill. So we went back to slowly towing a trailer by tractor through deep water and mud for fifty miles from Caia, which had an airfield that JAM, the United Nations and other agencies could use.

Heidi and I also landed at the Chupanga camp, between Marromeu and Caia. Its dirt runway had been marked unusable on charts for many years, but it had recently been graded, so we tried it. The surface had not yet been compacted, and after a few hundred feet on the landing roll we started sinking into the mud, even with our oversize tires. It took twenty people to pull us out and turn us around for takeoff. Thick mud was splattered all over our wings by the wheels, even with mudflaps. In this and a neighboring camp we found eighteen thousand refugees out of food and virtually without medical care. Four hundred women were pregnant and about to give birth, all without nutrition and basic necessities. Supply trucks struggling over available roads were breaking down. One truck tried to get to Beira, the nearest city, by following railroad tracks and blew up on a land mine. Darryl Greig, an Australian on our staff, spent seven hours hauling four tons of food by tractor through the night from Caia, 25 miles away, but Chupanga needed many times that every day.

Three of our churches were now in the Chupanga camp, waiting for emergency aid. Again we met with our pastors and heard their stories. This year's flood was so different, because tens of thousands of these flood victims were from our own churches. Their leaders had been through our Bible school. We taught them to trust Jesus for everything, and now we were with them and could see what they faced. They lived in the dirt in donated tents and tarps spread over sticks. They tried to cook what hard, raw maize they got in pots over wood fires. They had almost nothing but the clothes they were wearing. Ongoing rain kept everything a wet, muddy mess.

In the evening we tried to show the *Jesus* film, but our generator's regulator broke, and runaway voltage blew up our sound system. We felt heavy oppression and demonic opposition all around us. Far into the night groups were beating their drums and dancing to their native rituals. We were exhausted, dirty and hungry. I collapsed onto the hard ground in our tent, and soon Heidi followed. It was so hot. Our mosquito bites were painful. We sprayed ourselves, and the bites stung all over. We just lay there perspiring, listening to the sounds of human suffering. We could hear hundreds of people coughing. So many people were sick with malaria, cholera, pneumonia and parasites. Then the rain started pouring again. We had given our tent's outer shell to Pastor Rego, our provincial leader who came with us, who only had a mosquito net for shelter. We put the shell back on our tent and moved Rego in with us. But the rain was so heavy that by morning the three of us, and our bags, papers and passports, were soaked. Water was running everywhere.

We had to make a long, sudden flight to South Africa to get a new generator and more supplies. But could we take off after all that new rain? Probably, if our plane wasn't too heavy. But now the camp wanted us to take two new passengers. A fourteen-year-old boy had fallen off a truck and broken his back. He lay in a tent in terrible pain and with no hope of treatment unless we got him out. We couldn't leave him in a city hospital alone, so his father had to come with him. We strapped everyone in, three people in two seats, spreading out a foam mattress behind the boy's back. He was hurting so much, and he had never been near a plane before. Yet again we were at full gross weight, only now we were straining through mud to take off. But with a little speed we lightened up, and the mud lost its grip on us. We lifted off and soared over the watery, wild plains of the Zambezi, glittering under the sun-freshened sky. With local rain squalls on all sides, we stayed at five hundred feet and darted our way between dark, nasty cells with ceilings right down to the ground. We made Beira in an hour, and I slowly helped our limping boy into the terminal and a taxi. He and his father had no way back, so we left them money and prayed our hearts out for them.

Then Heidi and I were back in the air for the three-hour flight to Nelspruit, South Africa. At ten thousand feet thunderstorms were still built up all around us, and I scanned my stormscope for safe routes. The skies were majestic beyond compare. Our God the master artist and craftsman painted cloud layers of every color and brightness, different every moment, across our path. Rivers and mountains came and went, and we never got tired of such raw, wild beauty. Our worship CD was on, and we simply talked with our Savior all the way. What are You doing in Africa, Jesus? What do You want to do through this flood? Take us; do anything You want with us. What do You want us to say to Your Body back home in America and all over the world? How do You want your Body to function in response to such indescribable need?

We did our business in Nelspruit in a single day, picked up another, smaller amplifier in Maputo and flew right back to the Zambezi, this time with a doctor and a nurse. In Chupanga we set up for our meeting all over again as Heidi interceded intensely in her tent. We spread a big sheet between two trees so thousands of people could see the *Jesus* film from both sides. This time our generator worked perfectly. The sound was loud and clear for everyone, and we even had a soundtrack in the local Sena dialect. We preached, and again everyone who heard wanted Jesus. Pastor Surpresa, our national director, was with us, and he stayed in the camp for several days, teaching and praying with the people as we continued to fly to other locations.

Then we had to get back to Maputo, far to the south, for our Bible school's graduation service, and we had to bring Surpresa, who was still at Chupanga, with us. But it had been storming at Chupanga for days, and its dirt strip, already marginal, was getting even softer. Other relief planes were sitting on the ground at Beira, waiting for the ceiling at Caia to lift, and no one else was going to Chupanga. I would at least get there, skim the field and see what it looked like. Again we dodged and punched through the rain at low level and found the little city of blue and white tents at the flood's edge. We floated down and buzzed the runway just to one side, taking a careful look at the watery streaks and tire marks. I checked the wind and made a careful approach from the river, ready to gun the engine and lift off again at the slightest sign of stickiness or uneven tracking. The flare was good, and we touched down lightly, finding that the sand and gravel in the soil had drained enough water and that the surface was just hard enough in the center of the runway. We stopped far short of the seriously muddy far end of the runway, and a huge crowd from the camp ran out to meet us. Surpresa was grinning broadly, full of the joy of the Lord as always and very glad to see us. He had been ministering constantly, always with a crowd around him. A priest in the camp was angry with him, though, because some sick people wanted prayer instead of medical treatment.

We unloaded one passenger, reloaded our sound and camping equipment, and Surpresa, Darryl and I lifted off over the Zambezi again for another staggeringly spectacular African sunset stroked from God's endlessly varied palette of sky, clouds and water. We dropped into Caia to confer with pastors, and then right at sundown we headed into solid rain and clouds at four thousand feet back to Beira, where Heidi was waiting for us. Rain beat hard on our windshield in the black night, but the turbulence was mercifully light. Villages, forests, lakes and wild animals slipped below us unseen as we traveled in one hour what would take a truck nineteen hours in normal conditions. Rain still obscured the lights of Beira as we got close, and we didn't have a clear view of the runway until we were almost finished with our instrument approach.

The next day, and after another flight, we were back in Maputo. Our pastors, most of them from the north beyond the Zambezi, graduated. Over and over the Holy Spirit filled them to overflowing. They burned with zeal to spread the Gospel throughout the north, one of the most terribly poverty-stricken areas on earth. Our trucks took them as far toward home as possible, and then they had to ride whatever transport they could find from river to overflowing river. Many ended their trips on canoes across the Zambezi, carrying the precious plastic bags of food we sent with them.

In all this hardship our churches kept growing everywhere in the flood. They took in hundreds of orphans. They baptized new believers, even in dirty water full of leeches. The disaster did not turn the people of northern Mozambique away from God, but instead caused them to cry out for Him alone. They knew their sin. They knew they deserved nothing. But God revealed His grace as He has to few people anywhere. May His people here shine His light on the Western church and on hearts all over the world that need His perspective and love.

I was thirsty and you gave me drink—June 2001

Nampula's lights finally appeared dead ahead in the fading sunset as we descended out of the clouds. We had followed the coast up from the Zambezi and then turned inland toward the rocky hills of Mozambique's northern interior, a thousand miles from our base in Maputo. The runway lights blazed brightly, standing out from the town's dim streets. I circled our Cessna to land into the wind, and we settled into yet another airport, saving days and days of struggling through deep mud and torn-up roads with a four-wheel-drive truck. Heidi, Guy Chevreau, our speaker from Canada, and I climbed out, so glad to move and stretch after being squeezed in by baggage and sound equipment. We were there to meet with our newest pastors, who had planted twelve churches in the last three months to extend our presence into this huge province for the first time.

The airport was nearly deserted, but finally some of our pastors emerged from the terminal where they had been wait-ing for hours. We telephoned for taxis, and eventually a couple of battered, smoking, misfiring cars showed up and we headed for our conference center. This was not a hotel ballroom, boardroom, carpeted sanctuary or even a warehouse. It was one of our churches that we just sent up money to build. We pulled up, began to unload our stuff in the dark and tried to find a place for it all inside. Our people were eagerly crowding all around, trying to help. Our "church" turned out to be a big mud-and-stick hut, dusty and stuffy inside, with just a couple of dim candles to cast a glow over the faces of our brand-new African family in Jesus.

In the shadowy, flickering light, we saw old men quietly

staying back, ladies resting on straw mats laid over the dirt floor, children shyly inching closer and our pastors huddling on rough wooden benches, waiting patiently together to hear us speak. We were finally there, and we began to talk, asking them about their needs and expectations.

They were hungry, tired and penniless. This was our first conference in Nampula Province, a major event. Some of our pastors had walked from their villages for two days without food to get here, sleeping on the dirt by the side of the road at night. Others walked four days, and one six days—to learn from us. All came with only the poor, threadbare clothes on their backs. Now they were all waiting to see what we would do. Guy asked them, "What are you most afraid of?" "That our children will starve to death while we are here," they answered simply. They didn't even know how they would survive going home. What did we have to say?

Heidi and I deliberately came to Mozambique to face situations like this. We came to test the Gospel and strip from our preaching everything that didn't work and wasn't the Truth. We came to give people the living Jesus, not to try out our mission strategy on them. We came to love the poorest of the poor into the Kingdom, not to promise them a cheap road to health and wealth. We came asking Jesus to kill us, destroy us and remake us however He wanted so that we would be useful to Him here. And now we faced the test.

These people were suffering. They were sick and weak. They had seen their children die in their arms. Muslims persecuted them. They saw no hope outside the Good News we brought. So we preached the purest, simplest messages we could, straight from Scripture. We had no confidence in any other ideas we might have. They needed words that the Holy Spirit would back up. They needed to know what Jesus will bless and support, what will attract His company and presence. They needed content they could depend on to the death.

Their simple backgrounds were littered with witchcraft, syncretism, folk stories and petty religious legalism passed down from centuries of colonialism. Their cultural traditions left them exposed to inefficiency and immorality. Lack of viable government leadership and medical services in the bush deprived them of benefits we take for granted every day. Our pastors could read, haltingly, but most of their people could not. They could hardly picture the outside world, much less the Israel of Bible times. But one thing they knew: They wanted this Jesus we preached!

For the next few days Heidi, Guy and I alternated, pouring ourselves out the best we could through struggling interpreters. Makua, one of Mozambique's several dozen major languages, was spoken there. The pastors were eager, soft and responsive, even as they were weighed down by hardship. We laid hands on them and prayed for them, and the Holy Spirit richly moved on many. They didn't want us to go. They wanted to know so much more. They wanted us to be with them and to show them the way. We knew only Jesus could do that, but we were His voice, hands and feet.

We supplied money for fish and rice, and each day big pots were cooking over wood fires in the dirt courtyard by the church. The pastors were desperate for their own Bibles, so we went through town and located enough sources to get one for each, either in Portuguese or Makua. We bought bicycles and enough plastic tarp to cover every church.

One night we had a crusade meeting in a big, central dirt square surrounded by poor huts and crowds of people. We tacked a sheet up on a brick wall, hooked up our video projector, started our generator and showed the *Jesus* film in Makua. Everyone gathered around. Children stopped their running and playing, teenage boys forgot their soccer game and adults pressed in. This was Muslim territory. It takes years to convert a few dozen people, we were told. But no one wanted to miss the film. We could hardly maintain control. At the end we preached again, asking who wanted this Jesus, the Savior of the world. Everyone, absolutely everyone—and another thousand people bowed their hearts before the King.

Our work in Maputo continued along with our expansion in the north. Prostitutes on the streets gave up their way of life to live with us. Almost every day Heidi brought in more children, all without anyone else in their lives to love or care for them. Our churches around the country began to catch this same vision, bringing in the orphaned and abandoned, building simple mud-and-stick houses for them and learning to provide for them by faith in spite of their own great poverty.

Many visitors flew in to spend time with us, and every day we were asked, "How can we help?" Our answer was always the same: Very simply, you can always love and hug children. And you can spend a few weeks of your life to get a glimpse of how much of the world lives—and let your heart break. But more deeply, in order for you to be useful to the Master here—or anywhere—you must be close to Him and in love with Him. To the degree that you are intimate with Him, you will know what to do, what you must do. Jesus says drastic things in Scripture, such as, "You still lack one thing. Sell everything you have and give to the poor, and you will have treasure in heaven. Then come, follow me" (Luke 18:22).

We need to know what He is telling each of us specifically. Do you want to love Him and to be blessed by His presence? Here in Africa, He is all around us. He is poor, sick, naked and hungry. And as we get intimate with Him, we find ourselves taking care of Him, and He will say on that Great Day, "Come, you who are blessed by my Father; take your inheritance, the kingdom prepared for you since the creation of the world. For I was hungry and you gave me something to eat, I was thirsty and you gave me something to drink, I was a stranger and you invited me in, I needed clothes and you clothed me, I was sick and you looked after me, I was in prison and you came to visit me" (Matthew 25:34–36).

Our faith and religion are worthless if we do nothing about the physical needs of those who suffer from poverty (see James 2:16). We preach the Word, we bring the gifts of the Spirit, we celebrate and worship, we press on toward eternal life, fishing for the souls of people everywhere, but Jesus can tell if we love Him. Will we even bring Him just a cup of cold water when He is thirsty?

A conference at Morrumbala—August 2001

"Nothing's getting across the Zambezi," Darryl announced over the phone. "The ferries aren't running, and I had to drive my Isuzu back down the Caia road. The truck got so damaged I barely made it home!" Our Morrumbala conference plans were already in pieces. Without our trucks, we were going to have to fly all of us and our equipment across the river.

We got our team of pastors past the Zambezi to Quelimane by commercial plane, and I hauled the generator and all the sound gear I could in our Cessna. We managed to hire a beat-up van to take most of the team to Morrumbala, and then I flew another full load. I touched down onto weeds and rocks just before sunset the night of our first meeting. The airstrip had hardly been used in years. We were in remote Africa, far from hotels and restaurants, surrounded by the silent suffering of poverty. Mozambique's civil war was cruel to Morrumbala, a frequent battleground. Many died, leaving many more orphans. And now floods, hunger and disease bore down on the people with even more cruelty.

Hundreds of children in their rags jumped and shouted all around us as we unloaded. "The missionaries have come!" This was a big night for our churches all across Zambezia Province. Pastors traveled on foot and by local transport for days to join us. They were so excited, so encouraged. Jesus did not forget them. They were part of His Body, linked together in spirit and love across huge distances. In Him they found family! They had wanted this conference for so long.

We moved into simple guest rooms at a World Vision compound, a huge help to us. Soon the van arrived after a long, rough trip, and our team was together again. The sky darkened and the stars of the southern hemisphere enriched the heavens in their vast array. The town was dim. The air cooled down. There was no arena or auditorium. We walked out onto a dirt field nearby to see what had been set up for us. Thousands had already arrived from the bush, and they were cooking maize in big pots over wood fires. That night they would have to huddle on straw mats laid out on the dirt under trees or in a bombed-out building by the field with no roof. They had no changes of clothes. There was no running water, and there were no bathrooms or showers. They didn't even have toothbrushes or towels. They lived with sweat and dirt, decaying teeth, sickness and running sores. The night would be cold, but they came for the fire of the Holy Spirit.

Some crude planks were nailed together for a speaking platform in the center of the field and covered by plastic sheeting for protection from the next day's sun. Crowds surged toward us, trying to see what we were doing. We placed our generator far off to one side and ran a long cord to the platform. Everyone wanted to see the *Jesus* film that first night, so somehow in the darkness and all the confusion we strung up a king-size bedsheet for a screen and set up the projector and sound system. Thick, blowing dust was kicked up by tramping feet. Someone had mislabeled the videotape and we had the wrong dialect, but the people understood enough and wanted us to show it anyway. The video plug was intermittent, and the screen kept going blank. Everyone desperately wanted to see the movie, and they pressed in and fell over each other. Children were under my feet and everywhere. Pastors were trying to keep the crowd under control. I struggled to keep the video working. This event was unimaginably rare and special, and no one wanted to miss out.

Just before the end, the projector quit completely, but we turned on a floodlight and started preaching anyway. Again everyone wanted Jesus. There was shouting, cheering, singing and praying. Out of disorder came a huge cry for the King. He is the hope of Mozambique, the only salvation for these destitute people so poor in spirit. In all the noise and tumult, Jesus was finding lost sheep, and He will hold them safely in His heart forever.

Eventually, there was quiet and we could tear down for the night. I walked back to our compound, exhausted. It was impossible for so many people to see such a video properly. But hunger for God had broken out, and Zambezia would not be denied the Gospel. For the rest of our three days in Morrumbala, our team preached and taught—in the hot sun, in the dark night, at every available moment. No one resisted the Gospel. Children eagerly gathered to hear Bible stories, and the sick were brought to us for prayer. Passionately our speakers imparted a pastor's heart to our church leaders in the bush. The Holy Spirit swept through the meetings, and with shaking, weeping and loud cries, the hungry threw themselves before God. They needed Him, they wanted Him, they loved Him, and He loved them back. Hearts were filled, energy and initiative rose up, visions were granted and healings were reported. A girl deaf and dumb from birth spoke for the first time, and her family and friends sang and danced all the way back to their village.

We moved on to yet another conference to the south at Dondo. Again we saw revival and the intense hunger for God that swept this country. Our pastors did another careful count of our churches, and we found that we had more than three thousand, including those in Malawi and South Africa— a thousand more than we realized. We counted as a church a group of more than fifty, and these churches usually included as many as could hear a preacher's voice without a sound system— three hundred or more. We were approaching the point of having a church in every single village in large areas of central Mozambique and southern Malawi. Pastors were calling us from other countries—Ghana, Kenya, Tanzania, Zimbabwe— wanting the same revival. Our leading evangelists could not wait to get to Angola and Sudan.

We are asked how we can continue doing such tiring work. How do we put up with such poverty and stressful conditions? How can we deal with so many people and needs? How long can we do this? But we have nothing to gain by slowing down and trying to hold on to our lives. We give ourselves as a fragrant offering of love to Jesus, and in return He gives us His supernatural life. We have to stand up and face some of the poorest people on earth, who suffer, starve and die as most of us cannot imagine. Yet we can confidently preach: "Who shall separate us from the love of Christ? Shall trouble or hardship or persecution or famine or nakedness or danger or sword? As it is written: 'For your sake we face death all day long; we are considered as sheep to be slaughtered.' No, in all these things we are more than conquerors through him who loved us. For I am convinced that neither death nor life, neither angels nor demons, neither the present nor the future, nor any powers, neither height nor depth, nor anything else in all creation, will be able to separate us from the love of God that is in Christ Jesus our Lord" (Romans 8:35–39).

We have His love. We have Him! This is no time to be conservative. This is no time to let our hearts be captured by this world. We cannot improve on His will and His life. Let's concentrate on what captures God's attention and spend ourselves as He spends Himself. He knows what is worthwhile to do, so let's learn from Him and not waste our lives. We will never run dry. We always have His resources, because He died for us. Let's run the race to win and never stop bearing fruit.

Chapter 8

Stop for the Dying

We should stop every single time for each person.

Charlotte was another person, just a precious little boy who had been raped, beaten and broken, sick with pneumonia, dying on the street. All I (Heidi) know to do is to stop each time. Not just walk by, but stop. So we brought Charlotte home, but he wasn't able to talk. He would cry all the time—just cry, cry, cry. I found him downtown at night with a couple of other kids around him. He was really weak from the pneumonia and was just lying on the ground. He could hardly walk, he was so weak. Our Dr. Bob from New York was with us, and he said Charlotte's pneumonia was extremely severe.

We would hold him and rock him in our arms and just keep loving him. And he was healed—he was healed of his pain, his agony, his pneumonia. It took about six weeks to see his spirit start to recover, and after a couple of months he began getting better physically. But Charlotte really turned around when Pastor José, who started to minister with us, decided to receive Charlotte as his own child. Almost every weekend José takes him home to his own house and has a special time of love just with him.

Another child, Jito, was diagnosed with AIDS and living on the streets. Jito was robbing, stealing, always pushing and hitting everybody and continuously in need of love. But as we kept on loving and loving Jito, the Lord touched him. He was healed of AIDS and got a negative test back from the doctor. Pastor José also takes Jito home on the weekends, so Jito and Charlotte feel the love of a father, a Mozambican father who cares for them.

As I saw this happening, I was praying about what we were supposed to do. The Lord had showed me thousands and thousands of children, and I believe we are called to care for millions of children. At first I was absolutely overwhelmed with that vision, and I thought, "God, how could that ever happen? How could we ever do that, just stopping for the one? I don't see how we could ever, ever do that." I was praying, crying, fasting and asking God, and He said that He would bring a great revival, and in this revival He would touch the hearts of the pastors, and they would become fathers of the fatherless. He said that was His answer for these children. They would be literally cared for by these Mozambican pastors. And then He told me that the widows would cook for them and feed them, that the widows would help farm and that we were to build indigenous buildings made of mud and straw, buildings that fit in with every church. We would see these children cared for in families.

So José was one of the first pastors to start taking kids home. Pastor Rego also started taking kids home, and then other pastors did as well. Now many, many pastors are taking in children, anywhere from one to ten. We've asked them all to pray to take in one to ten. The Lord is multiplying the revival, and now our mission has over five thousand churches in ten countries. We've asked every church to take in children. So I believe this will be the way that these orphans and street children, and all the children with AIDS, will be cared for in family units.

It's wonderful to watch these pastors come for their training at Zimpeto. They come to study the Bible (Old and New Testaments), theology and spiritual disciplines. But they also learn about caring for orphans and widows. When they arrive, the first thing they see is hundreds and hundreds of children living with us. We tell them, "This is the heart of Jesus, and Jesus told us there would always be enough, because He died. You, too, can take in children. It doesn't matter that you're poor. It doesn't matter that you might not have money. If you will believe God to take in one, and then two and then three, God will give you more and more faith to take them in." The glorious thing is, these pastors are taking them in on their own initiative as Jesus touches their hearts.

Charlotte and Jito are wonderful prototypes of this kind of ministry. Hundreds and hundreds of children have followed and are now in family units and churches. We believe that if every church all over Africa and India, every church that faces orphans, AIDS and the poor, would just believe God and take in a few, then we can take care of every child. They will be in homes, they will be loved and they will be blessed. They will not be fatherless. The Bible says that the Lord will gather the fatherless into families and He will care for them and minister to them. That's what we are seeing, so we're blessed. Praise God!

The heart of Jesus is multiplied as our visitors walk with us among the poor. We have over a thousand visitors a year coming through. We take them all out to the streets and dumps, and wherever God is pouring out His Spirit in the north, south, east and west, they're seeing the heart of Jesus being poured out.

Recently when we've gone to the streets, we've been ministering first at Costa do Sol, where prostitutes are living in a halfway-house situation. They're selling their bodies. They're as young as nine years old. It's called *campismo,* a camping ground at Costa do Sol. These girls sleep on the floor in an old room. So we've been going there with staff from around the world, and with Zacharias and Louis, who were both street kids themselves. Zacharias was a gang leader and a bandit, and he was powerfully saved on the street. He fell on his knees and met Jesus, came to work with us in Zimpeto and was transformed by the Lord. He learned to read and write, and he is now one of our best street preachers. Every Sunday morning he goes to the streets with Louis, Evan and some of our kids, and they minister there. Tuesdays we go back. This is just a camping ground. There's a fire burning. Little kids and prostitute girls all gather around. Young men and teenage boys with no jobs are also selling themselves. We just begin to pray, worship and call on the Lord.

One week I was just so sad that every week they would pray, but none of them had given up their lifestyles. I cried out to God, and they all came to Zimpeto that Sunday for one of our big wedding feasts. We take Scripture literally: "But when you give a banquet, invite the poor, the crippled, the lame, the blind, and you will be blessed. Although they cannot repay you, you will be repaid at the resurrection of the righteous" (Luke 14:13–14). We send out our four-ton trucks and pick up the poor, the sick, the bandits, all the desperate people we can find, and bring them to church.

This particular Sunday the prostitutes came. Guy Chevreau was preaching. I felt the burden of Jesus in my heart. I was so sad they hadn't changed their lifestyles even though they had met Jesus. So I said, "Now, come forward if you really want to change." They ran forward to be purified, to be clean. I said, "Now is the day of your deliverance. Now is the day God's going to set you free." I was on a forty-day fast, and my heart was broken for these girls. I began crying out, "Lord, do it now. Do something now!" I know only the Holy Spirit can really change hearts. There's nothing we can do, but the Holy Spirit can do it. So I said, "If you really want to change, if you really want a new life, if you really want to stop being prostitutes, then just kneel down and ask God to make a way when there is no way."

I didn't even know what way He would make, because I didn't know what to do with them. I knew I couldn't bring nine-year-old or even fifteen-year-old prostitutes into Zimpeto. I knew we needed another place to put them, but we didn't have the staff, and we were already overstretched and over-exhausted. I didn't know what to do, but I knew God knew what to do. I remember every time Jesus saying, "Heidi, there's enough, because I died." And so I stretched out again and believed God. These girls started weeping and crying, and the next Tuesday when we arrived for our street outreach, they literally came running to me. They fell and knelt down in the sand and said, "Mama, we can't live this way anymore. We're ready to change. We want to change. We don't want to keep selling ourselves. We don't want to die of AIDS. We don't want to die of gonorrhea and syphilis. We want to follow Jesus. We don't want to leave His presence anymore. We have to know Him. We have to follow Him. This is no life. There's no life here. We can't stand it anymore." After about a year of being at *campismo,* that day everything changed for these girls. Glory to God!

Later another seven girls came off the street. Evan, who danced with angels in visions and sat on Jesus' lap when he was still stealing and ready to run back to his old life, is now preaching with Zacharias and Pedro out there on the streets. They are bringing in these girls. We prayed and prayed about what to do. We started building simple, little houses in a community near our center. Some of these girls came to our school, and we started cottage industries for others. Lucia, our first woman pastor besides myself, felt led to move out there and pastor these girls. And then when this miracle happened and they all wanted to come off the streets at once, we were really overwhelmed, and we didn't know what to do. But God knew what to do. It had to be an instant answer from Jesus.

We began to pray and ask God for another pastor. I was thinking it must be someone from our Bible school, someone trained, someone who could read, speak proper Portuguese and disciple the girls in the Word. And here was Louis, who had been living on the street for probably four years or so. He had been burned in a cardboard house. Some people he thought were his friends poured gasoline all over his cardboard hut in the street and tried to burn him to death. They locked him in behind a flimsy door, and he couldn't get out. He almost died and has scars all over his body. He'd been in the hospital for a long time, and I met him on the street after he got out. He cried and wept and met Jesus. I told him how Jesus would forgive his sins, love him and care for him, and I told him all about His mercy and grace. Louis taught me so much about forgiveness, because one of the first things Louis said to me was, "Well, I need to go forgive all my friends. I need to talk to them about Jesus' love and mercy and just forgive all of them who tried to burn me to death." He's done that, and he's been preaching on the streets for years now.

So as we were praying for a pastor to help these street girls, the Lord just spoke to my heart, "Louis." He'd never been to school. He couldn't read or write until we got him into one of our literacy programs. He'd never had a Bible school class. He was just working in our construction department. I went over to him at *campismo* and said, "Louis, do you think Jesus could use you to help pastor these girls with Lucia?" Louis began to weep. He just began to cry in the sand. We didn't have buildings. We were out there in the sand under the trees, and he began to cry, tears dripping into the sand, running down his face and down his scarred hands. And he said, "Oh, Jesus would honor me with such a thing? Jesus would let me do such a thing for Him? Of course. What joy, what great joy! Of course I'll go. Oh, I would love to go. I would love to pastor these girls and the orphans from the floods." And Louis is out there with Lucia, ministering.

So we found that those who are most broken, most abused, most outcast become some of the most anointed ministers we have out of thousands of churches. They seem to be the ones who run ahead of all the rest of the pastors. They run ahead in mercy; they run ahead in grace; they run ahead because they know what it is to live under a bridge; they know what it is to be beaten, to be raped, to be burned, cold and hungry. They're the ones who have compassion for the homeless and broken, for the prostitutes, for the ones out there, and they teach us every day more and more of the love of Jesus. I pray Jesus will keep sending us more people like Louis, Zacharias, Evan and Pedro who move in the power and mercy of God.

Many people in the Church are frustrated because they don't

see a harvest. They're frustrated because they have so little fruit, and they wonder why. They keep going to the same people. In the parable of the great banquet in Luke 14:15–24, the rich didn't want to come. They were busy enjoying their money and possessions, and they made excuses. The poor can't do these things, and they are eager to come to the banquet when they are invited. God says there are no excuses, but the Church keeps going to the wealthy and well-fed, and then it wonders why they don't respond.

God is saying, "Wake up, Church! Wake up, Church! The Church isn't ready for the wedding feast. The poor need to be called." The Lord is looking for servant-lovers who are passionate for Him, who are filled with love for Him, who are longing for the Bridegroom's return, who can taste the feast and know it's about to begin. They can't stand anymore to stay in their comfort, to wait around for someone to be saved. They will literally run out and call in the poor, the crippled, the blind and the lame. If we will go, they will come.

I've never met a person since we've been in Mozambique who hasn't said yes to Jesus. The poor come by the hundreds, by the thousands, by the hundreds of thousands. They come one by one, because they know they're hungry. There's something about the poor that delights the heart of God. They're contrite. They know they're in need. What is it about the poor that makes them want to come to Jesus? What is it about the poor that literally brings the Kingdom of God, that allows them to experience the Kingdom of God in a way that the well-fed don't? It has to do with hunger. It has to do with their need. They know they need God. They're hungry and thirsty. The Lord wants to cause even the rich, even the middle-class, to be poor in spirit and know that they are in need of Him.

The poor teach us how to seek after God. The poor teach us how to long for God and how to forgive. The poor teach us more about God's heart because they have to depend on Him. God wants us to be dependent on Him at all times. The poor are always hungry. God is calling us to hunger and thirst after Him. The poor are thirsty. The Lord is calling us to thirst after

Him. The poor will never say no to a feast. They'll come and eat. The Lord is setting out spiritual banquets for His Church, but so many are just full. They have smorgasbords and buffets and restaurants at every corner. They're just not hungry.

The Lord is calling for servant-lovers who will call in the outcasts, who will go into the dark corners of the world and compel the poor to come. And they will come. They'll come by the millions. Who will go and leave their lives of comfort and call in the broken? Who will go and be a learner? Who will go and lay their lives down for Jesus among the poor? The Lord Jesus wants His house to be full. It's time for us to go out to the poor, to the broken, to the homeless, to the dying and to the lonely and call them to come in. Thousands and thousands of missionaries and ministers need to go out to the darkest places, to the poorest places, to the forgotten places, because the wedding feast is about to begin and so many of the poor haven't been called. Rush out and call them. They will come.

Every Friday near the dump we build houses or put roofs on houses. The poorest of the poor build shacks out of junk and scraps, and sometimes they find enough trash and straw to build walls, but they could never come up with enough money, even in a hundred years, to put tin roofs on their houses. Such money is beyond them. It would be like a million dollars for someone else. It's an impossible dream. We were praying about what to do as we saw Jesus walking on the dump, transforming the poor and calling them to the wedding feast. They scavenge in the dump twelve hours a day, and then they go home and try to rest on a dirt floor in a sagging, leaking hut reeking of garbage. We prayed, "What can we do, Jesus? What can we do until You come back and have these people sit in the front like You showed us? What can we do until they have the literal robes on them? What can we do now? We pray, 'Your Kingdom come, Your will be done on earth as it is in heaven.' So what can we do now for these people?" And that's always our big struggle. What can we do now, not just in heaven?

We decided we could build one or two houses every week with the help of the brothers, the youth that got saved in the dump. We provide the roof material, and they provide all the labor. Antonio was desperate. He said, "Mama, I really want to get married. I really want to have a life. I have no life. I have no house. I have nothing. I love Jesus, but I have nothing. I love Jesus, but I have nowhere to sleep. I love Jesus, but I have no possibility of ever getting married, because I have no place to bring a wife. And I just want a life where I can be married and have children and love God." And he said his brothers had given him a little piece of land. It was in the garbage dump. It was still wet from the rain and a bit muddy. Two years later the lot right next door was still full of water from the flooding, because the poor always have the worst land. So he said, "I really, finally got a little piece of land. I would just love to build a house." We were able to get all the straw and sticks to make this house, and about ten of the youth sang, danced, cheered and started to build. Vacinto was sitting on the truck and he just said, "Wow, Mama, this is an amazing day. This is a glorious day. Look, I never would have imagined that Antonio would ever have a house. God is God. Look at what He's done! Antonio's going to have a house. God loves us! God is powerful. God is awesome. God really does care about us. God really does care about our suffering, because Antonio has a house. This God is God, and I want to love Him and follow Him forever."

And I just began to cry because he was so grateful for this little, straw house that his friend was going to have for the first time. And all the youth worked all day long to build this house in the hot sun. They were the most joyful bunch of guys, building this house for Antonio. You know, it's not just about seeing them saved. It's about seeing their whole lives transformed by God's love. It's not just loving with words. Don't just love with your words, but love with your actions.

The same day another lady said, "Mama Aida, please come visit my husband. You prayed for my daughter and my son who had malaria and cholera, and as you said, they were instantly healed. They're fine and they're healthy. It's a total miracle that they're completely healed. But my husband's been paralyzed for two years. He hasn't walked for two years. Can you please come and pray for him?" So I started following her down the little sticker bush pathways with garbage everywhere. She kept saying, "It's really close. It's really close."

But first we had to stop at another house where George lives. George is a big, tall man who's mentally retarded and unable to speak properly. His brain's not functioning very well, and he just kind of mumbles once in a while. We stopped at his house, which was just some straw without a roof and with a piece of board on the dirt. He said that's where he lives, and could we please cover his house, too? We knelt down, about five of the brothers and myself, in that pitiful place, garbage everywhere. They walk barefoot in the dirt and glass. The garbage dump never stops burning. There's always smoke. We just knelt down on his straw and prayed that Jesus will help him and give him a roof. And the following Friday the youth put a roof on George's house.

My friend kept saying, "Come on, come on! It's just a little further." It took about an hour to walk to her house. It was another little, straw hut, but she swept it clean and picked reeds from the floodwater to make a little mat for her husband to sit on. And there he was, sitting on a reed mat, unable to walk for two years. He had a pair of scissors in his hand, and he was cutting up little pieces of paper. I suppose he would make one cent in three hours, but he wanted to do something. He didn't want to sit and do nothing, so he was cutting paper to sell to the mattress vendors who would put these scraps into locally made mattresses for the poor. I prayed, "Jesus, what am I going to do for him? What do you want me to do?" As I prayed, the Lord said, "Baptize him."

I usually immerse people in water as we baptize them, but there was no water for that around. So I thought, "Well, I've heard the Lord," and I took a cup of water and asked him if I could baptize him. He said, "Yes, I would love to be baptized." I took this cup and in the name of the Father, the Son and the Holy Spirit, I baptized Carlos. And then I laid my hands on his head and said, "In the name of Jesus, get up. Get up, Carlos, and walk. In the name of Jesus I break the evil curse over you and your family. I break your paralysis, and I pray for Jesus to come, for the Holy Spirit to come and cause you to walk, in Jesus' name." I took his hand and said, "Now, stand up and walk."

For the first time in two years, Carlos got up! He stood up. The family started singing. The children started singing. People started gathering around, and Carlos walked around the house twice. It was the most glorious time. Later, his wife came back and said he walked to the bathroom and took a shower. He's walking totally on his own today, completely healed. The Kingdom is coming in the garbage dump. The Kingdom is coming for the poor. Jesus is healing them and pouring His love into them. Jesus cares for them.

We take in little children one by one, abandoned, broken children. Some are blind and deaf. Jesus heals some of them instantly. They see, and others don't see. Others stay with us blind but full of Jesus' love. I think some of them may see better than those whose eyes are opened, because they know about Jesus' love and they know about His presence. We take in children abandoned by their parents, left to scavenge in the dump alone, eight years old, nine years old, filled with soot and misery. We bring them home and love them, care for them and nurture them, and their lives are transformed. The great miracle is that the ones who were the bandits and thieves and tried to murder us are now our friends. Every Friday they help preach the sermon with me. We do drama. They illustrate it. They lead worship. They clean out our little church in the dump. They're filled with His joy and presence. They're filled with Him. Their lives have truly been transformed by the love of God. Out of all the churches that I know, our dump church is definitely one of my favorites, because I know that one day the poorest of the poor will sit in the front at the wedding supper of the Lamb. I know that not one of them will ever make an excuse, but that they will always desperately want to come and eat with Jesus, dance with Jesus, live with Jesus and love Jesus. They know that He is all they have and all they need.

There's something very powerful about baptisms that we

overlook at times. When our girls who have been prostitutes get baptized, demons go crazy as soon as their toes hit the water. They try to drown the girls by flipping them to one side and turning them under the water. They start screaming and thrashing. There's something demons can't stand about baptism, because it represents a person who will no longer live for the devil, a person who has surrendered to Jesus. We gently take hold of a girl's head and say, "In the name of Jesus we bind you, Satan, and tell you demons to be still and quiet." As we baptize them one by one, the girls are made calm. Sometimes it takes a bit of struggle, but they calm down. We ask them to forgive all the men who have abused them and slept with them, who have beaten them, hurt them and made them miserable, even their own fathers. And these little girls, some nine, ten and twelve years old, begin to forgive. We say, "Give them a gift, even a gift they don't deserve, the gift of love, the gift of mercy, the gift of forgiveness." As these girls begin to forgive their abusers, the demons flee from their hearts, and they are set free. We put them under the baptismal water, and they come out clean and pure. Their lives are made new.

Other children, without anyone telling them what's going to happen, begin to pray in tongues as they come out of the water, and they often fall back into the water under the weight of God's glory in that baptismal tank. There is such a powerful presence of God in that tank. Mozambican pastors baptize with us, and as the children come out of the tank, we see the sunlight on their faces. They begin to open their mouths, lift up their little hands and pray in tongues, in heavenly languages that they never learned. They're filled with the Spirit of the living God as they come out of those waters. It is glorious and powerful.

Probably like many reading this book, I have received prophecies for years that in our ministry the blind will see, the deaf will hear, the crippled will walk, the dumb will speak, the dead will be raised and the multitudes will come to Jesus. As time went on it seemed these prophecies became stronger. People began to minister those words over me more and more.

I especially remember Randy Clark prophesying over me in 1998. After that I would literally go out and look for every blind person I could find. Living in one of the poorest nations on earth, they're pretty easy to find. There are blind people all over, so I'd go up and just grab them and say, "I know you don't know me, but I'd just like to pray for you." I'd pray for them and I'd lead them to Jesus. Every one of them would get saved. I never felt like I failed because they came to Jesus, every one, but none of them saw. I must have prayed for twenty blind people, and none of them saw. But I kept praying. I kept remembering those prophetic words that the Holy Spirit poured into my heart. There was such a powerful presence of the Holy Spirit as those words were spoken over me. I just said, "I'm not giving up. I'm not giving up. One day they're going to see."

Tanneken Fros, one of our long-term missionaries, and I were in a little, mud church up north. We began to pray for another blind lady, and she fell onto the ground. Her eyes went from white to gray to brown, and she was healed and seeing. Her name was Aida, the same name that I have in Mozambique. We were so excited. We could hardly wait to pray for the next blind person. As we left that little mud church, everyone was singing, dancing and jumping. They were so thrilled. Demons were cast out, people were saved, more were healed, and as a result that whole community moved into revival. As we were leaving Aida was still on the ground, unable to get up, but she was seeing and she was happy. She was so overcome by the presence of God and by the weight of His glory upon her. For a long time she was unable to walk, but she could see, and the joy of the Lord was all over her face.

Next we prayed for another blind man on the street in a wheelchair, deformed by a large and terrible tumor on his head. I thought, "Surely he's going to see just like Aida." But he didn't see. Dr. Bob, who came all the way from America, was able to remove his tumor surgically and minister God's love to him. I led him to Jesus, and also his son, who pushed his dilapidated wheelchair. He immediately went into Pastor

Rego's church and was at our next conference, loving and honoring Jesus. His tumor is gone because of the love of a Christian doctor. His heart is filled with the love of Jesus, and I think even though he can't see physically, I know this man sees more than many of us see.

Tanneken and I were together the first three times we saw the blind see in Mozambique. We were in Pastor Rego's mud hut, praying for another blind lady, again named Aida. Both of us felt the compassion of God, and when we began to cry over her, she opened her eyes and said, "You're wearing a black shirt." We were so excited we hardly knew what to do. We asked, "How do you know it's black?" She answered, "Because I can see. I can see!" She went blind when she was eight years old, so she knew her colors. She knew I was wearing a black T-shirt. We went outside in the sun. She began to squint and squeal, and say, "Oh! Oh!" Then we said, "Now we want you to walk to where the ducks are." But they were quacking, and Tanneken said, "Better not do that. The ducks are quacking! We need to find something that's not making any noise!" So we directed, "Walk to the bucket." So she started walking to the bucket. We added, "Walk to that mango tree over there," and there she'd go, walking to the mango tree. "How many fingers am I holding up?" "Five." "How many fingers am I holding up now?" "Seven." She was healed. The community went ballistic. They started running in from all over the place, leaping and jumping, dancing and singing. They changed the name of the church to "The Church of Miracles." The second Aida was miraculously healed.

We were ministering at a conference in Chimoio, and I felt like Jesus was going to do it again. There was a blind lady being led by a little boy, and we prayed for her. Down she went, stuck to the floor, unable to move. Her eyes went from white to gray to brown. She was healed. She began to cry, and she said, "Oh, look what Jesus did for me! Look what Jesus did! Jesus loves me! Jesus has had mercy on me! Jesus really, really cares about me. Now I don't have to beg. Now I don't have to do my farming on my hands and knees in the dirt, in the dark. Now I can see! I can see! I can go cut wood in the forest and sell it in the market. Now I don't have to be a beggar anymore. Jesus loves me. Jesus cares about me. He is God, and I will love Him forever."

We were in the remote town of Marromeu, ministering to desperately hungry flood victims. Kurt Erickson, a pastor and old friend from England, was with us. In our morning meeting in the town's central square, I had a word of knowledge that deaf ears were being opened. We only had about five hundred people there, which was a small crowd for that town. But the deaf began to hear. Their ears were opened up, and so everybody started talking about it and the word went all around. That day the people began walking through deep floodwaters to get to our meetings. Marromeu had been left out of flood relief efforts, but by divine appointment we were able to arrange a Jesus Alive flight. Their turboprop transport plane landed on Marromeu's wet, muddy field and brought tons of badly needed milled maize with supplements. The word went out, "This is a church that loves!" And more people streamed toward Marromeu.

That night when we had our meeting, maybe ten thousand people showed up who had heard about the miracles. They were so excited, and many, many thousands gave their hearts to Jesus. And then they came forward for prayer. They never have you pray for headaches first, or toe aches, or backaches. They start right away with the deaf, the dumb and the blind. A girl came to us. She was deaf and she was blind, and I thought, "Oh, Jesus." You can get a little nervous when there are thousands of people and the first person they bring you is both deaf and dumb. I just prayed a simple prayer. I remember I was just sitting on a chair—no big push 'em over, knock 'em down, yell and scream, put it on video approach. There was no video camera. There were no flashlights. There were no cameras. There was nothing, just the dark, the rain and thousands of people. The lights were going out, and I began to pray, "In Jesus' name, open her eyes. I break the curse of blindness. I break the curse of deafness over her." And suddenly her eyes opened up. Her ears opened up, and she smiled this beautiful smile. Her mother screamed and screamed, "My daughter's healed! My daughter's healed! Look what Jesus did. My daughter's healed! Now she can work. Now her husband can come back!" Her husband had left her because she was useless, but she was miraculously healed. She'd gone blind and deaf about a year and a half before this day, and they don't know why it happened. I think it was probably a witch doctor curse, because I felt led to break a curse over her. So God poured His love into her, and again a village heard. After that, Marromeu came to Jesus. It seemed like the whole town wanted Him!

The Maputo jail is another of my favorite places to minister, and the anointing there continues to increase. On one occasion the Holy Spirit fell among the prisoners, and every one of them gave his heart to God. As they sat and knelt in the dark, huddled in one room, with the strong smell of urine in the air, the Holy Spirit came, convicting these men of their sins and allowing them to feel the love of the Father.

Later that night as we ministered in broken-down buildings and on the streets, four precious treasures were plucked from the darkness, and they came home to live with us. We took them to our house, and our eight boys helped give them warm showers and new clothes for the first time in their lives. We prayed with them and tucked them into their new beds.

No matter how big the revival is or how many thousands of churches there are, we hear the Lord's voice again: Stop for the dying man, the dying woman, the dying child on the road. Pour my oil and wine into their sores. Pick them up and bring them home. He wants to put eye salve on the eyes of the Church. He wants us to stop for the one. He wants us to see the one. The face of revival! This is His heart. Let it beat in you.

Chapter 9

All Fruitfulness Flows
from Intimacy

This book is for You, Lord. Our work is for You. We live for You.
We're here for You. We have no reason to live without You.

Let Him love you. It's so much simpler than we thought. It's
time to be transformed by His love so that there is no fear in
you. Be wrecked for everything but His presence. Be so utterly
abandoned in His love.

God in His glory will pour and pour His presence into people
to the degree that entire nations will be transformed. He will
pour His love out like a river, like an ocean. Let Him kiss you
with the kisses of His mouth.

It's time to lie down and let God be God. He is mighty, and
nothing is impossible with Him. He wants to kiss His Church
and transform you with His love.

We are called to be carriers of His glory. It's not about
standing up and being an eloquent speaker. It's about being
so close to the heart of God that you know what He's thinking.
Then you're not afraid to go anywhere and say anything. The
Lord Himself will do anything for radical lovers. He captivates
us so that we can never go back. He wants to shatter your box.
Often your God is still too small. It's His time for whole
nations.

Lie down so that He can trust you with everyone. Then when you get up there is revival—when whole nations come to Him, falling on their faces. He changes us with one glance of His eyes, so that we are not afraid to be completely abandoned in His arms. Many want lots of power and anointing, but when you just lie down and let Him kill you, it's a good thing. He wants to love you to death.

We are finally realizing that we have failed and that we cannot bring about the kind of revival this world needs. In the secret place of Your heart, Jesus, we will rest. We will lie down. We will listen, until You tell us to stand up. When You tell us to stand up, we know that nations will come to You.

He's looking for union, not occasional worship, so that our natures are transformed. We must walk in His nature, and we must die daily.

Some people say, "Just get a grip. We've already done that." But it's a daily thing, a continual laying down. All fruitfulness flows from intimacy. There's no other place to get it. To the degree that we are united with the heart of Jesus, God will bring fruit in our lives. To the degree that you are in love with Him, you will be fruitful.

I (Heidi) don't know anything else. I'm so desperate to stay in this place of abandonment. From this place nothing is impossible. I only have one message—passion and compassion. We're passionate lovers of God, so that we become absolutely nothing. His love fills us. When it's time to stand up, God stands up with us. We focus on His face, never on our ministry, anointing or numbers.

All I want to do is love God and care for His people. I find them in the garbage, under trees, dying of AIDS. I'm just really simple. Jesus said, "Just look into My eyes," and everything completely changed. His eyes are filled with love and passion and compassion. Jesus always stops for the dying man, the dying woman and the dying child. That's all I know, passion and compassion. He calls me to love every single person I see every single day.

There are so many tired Christians and burned-out ministers.

Go, go, work, work, rah, rah. Why? We don't bear much fruit running around like that. But when you're filled with His passion, fruit happens.

Just focus on His face. You will only make it to the end if you can focus on His face. Focus on His beautiful face. You can't feed the poor, you can't go to the street, you can't see anything happen unless you see His face. One glance of His eyes, and we have all it takes to lie down. We're not afraid to die.

We give our offerings, but our offering is going to have to be us. We have to say, "Go ahead. Take me. Take everything." The deal is, you have to see His face. You have to be completely wrecked by His love so that you will hilariously give your life away. You start to love the people you didn't think you could ever love, even the mean ones. But you have to see His face.

Since that time when I saw His face, a nation is coming to Jesus. We have to see Him in His glory, mercy, beauty and love. And then we need to see Him in the poor, in the least of these.

But we can't make revival happen. I know about all that forty-day fasting stuff. I used to do it so I could pray in revival. Now I do it just so I can be hungry for God. I do it so I can be poorer and desperately hungry and so I can relate to the hunger of a lost and dying world. I do it so I feel their pain and their suffering when I live with them in tents and refugee camps. It's a whole different place, you see. I can't go back.

We need to be in that place. We're prisoners of love. Some people say, "Oh, how noble. You're a missionary." I'm just a prisoner of love. I don't have any choice. It is joy unspeakable and full of glory. The whole thing. Every part of it. Even as babies die in my arms, there is this incredible joy in my spirit, because they died being loved. They went straight from our love and the love of our precious workers from all over the world, and all the Mozambicans, hundreds of them, and they go right into the hands of Jesus. And He just keeps on loving them, even more than we could. That's joy. That's victory.

One week eight of our precious ones died. I was really tired. I didn't understand. I love them so much. It was just one after another. Why? What do I do? Jesus said, "Either way, you win, because you loved them to life." I got just a glimpse of the eternal. I got a picture of His arms opening wide to receive those babies and those teenagers and those pastors, and I said, "Wow, just take me! I am so ready!" I so want to be there, because I've seen His face. One glance of His eyes and you're wrecked forever.

His call is for all of our lives. He calls each of us to be an extravagant, hilarious love offering to Jesus. That's the place where I believe the glory comes. This glory of His presence that we are so desperate for, that we so need, that we're so crying out for, that we're so longing for, that we sing about, comes as we hilariously, totally and completely give away our entire being before Him. We are the sacrifices He ignites with His love, and His presence just falls. He just comes. He is looking for people who will carry His glory. He really, really is.

But you have to be dead in order to carry it. And when you carry the glory, you will carry it out to the poor, the broken, the dying and the lost. You will. That's the call. That's the heartbeat of Jesus, that we carry Him out to the broken. But you can't carry Him until you've seen His face. You have to know that holy place.

You go from the place where you say, "Oh, God. I'll write a check, but just don't make me go to Africa. Please, oh, God, don't make me sit in the dump. I'd love to write a check. Here it is. It's a lot. Just don't make me go there. I don't like bugs," to where you just say, "Oh, God, here I am. Take me anywhere. Take me, use me, break me, bruise me if need be, pour me out, fill me up, here I am. I'm an offering. I'm it. I'm the offering. Take me. Pick me up with Your glory and let me be a carrier of Your presence into the darkness. I know You love me, God, because I've seen Your face."

God wants to do signs and wonders like we've never seen, but we have to see His face. We have to see what He sees and feel what He feels. Otherwise, it's dangerous and frightening. He can only release His power and anointing to those who will lie down, who will say, "Only You," and stay that way every single day.

The only reason I even think of getting on more airplanes is that God spoke to me and said, "Tell the Church it's time to wake up!" So wake up, wake up, wake up, wake up, Church!

This new army doesn't get tired. You know why? They know how to lie down in His presence. They know how to rest in His arms. They know how to lay their heads on His chest and listen to His huge heart. They weep with Him over the dying, the crying, the broken, the abused and the lost. Do you really think you can work hard and start a revival? Just run out there and get them? You can't. But when Jesus shows His face and He breathes life into the dry, dry, bony Church, and that Church stands up full of His presence, carrying His glory, nobody can resist anymore!

I had a Technicolor vision in December of 2001 in the living room of our good friends John and Carol Arnott. I saw the whole earth encircled with chariots of fire, thousands and thousands of them. In them were the saints of God, two by two. Their bodies were transparent. Nothing was hidden. The riders had huge hearts, filling their chests from shoulder to shoulder, and I could see them beating. They held up gleaming, golden swords in their hands. Two white horses led each chariot. All the reins to the horses were gathered together and went straight up to heaven where I saw the Lord holding them with His left hand. The Lord held His right hand high and brought it forward and down with a loud cry, "Now!" The chariots began to take off, galloping across the earth. They were chariots of fire, the chariots of God carrying the glory of the Lord. Wherever the chariots went, the fire went.

At some places on the earth the people said, "No, we don't want the Lord." And in those places I saw the most hideous, disgusting darkness and depravity ever imaginable. But wherever the people responded to the presence of the Lord, the light became brighter and the ground became ablaze with fire. I saw that the sword is both mercy for those who receive and judgment for those who reject. I don't like judgment and never liked to preach judgment, but I've received the vision. There is judgment!

The Lord said that His glory will cover the earth like the waters cover the sea, and that this revival that began in the late 1990s will be known not for manifestations, but for intimacy unto harvest. The Lord asked, "Who will carry My glory to the ends of the earth and not touch it? Who will ride in My chariots of fire? Who will release complete control into My hands and let Me hold the reins? The time is now! The harvest is now! It's time to reap!"

After that vision I felt extremely happy, thrilled, excited— and sad and miserable at the same time. I would have to start leaving my Zimpeto children and the streets of Maputo. Since that time we've been traveling to many nations preaching the Gospel and ministering in signs and wonders, and we can only spend a third of our time at home in southern Mozambique.

And since that vision our churches jumped in number from two thousand to over five thousand between December 2001 and August 2002. We've been hungering for this revival our whole lives. We don't understand why God would choose us to be a part of it. We're humbled and amazed. Signs and wonders keep increasing.

One of our favorite and most memorable meetings was held in late October of 2001 in Dondo, central Mozambique. Marc Dupont prophesied about the end-time revival to the poor spreading from the West and covering the entire earth. We felt the glory of the Lord moving upon our property. We had no buildings or carpets. Our faces were in the dirt. Marc couldn't see because the glory was so bright, so I crawled up to the platform. I was unable to stand, because the weight of His glory was so heavy. I welcomed the Holy Spirit to do whatever He wanted. Nearly everyone fell to the ground. No one had touched them. The first person we prayed for was blind and deaf—and instantly healed. Demon spirits were cast out. No human effort was involved. Little children were on their backs or faces, waving their arms, crying or smiling, lost in visions and the things of God. It was an incredible, unforgettable time. After that the people got up so in love with the Lord and full of

Jesus and His goodness that they ran out and planted hundreds more churches.

The harvest is so ripe that we don't know how to train leaders fast enough. Recently we landed on an old, abandoned airstrip near Mutarara on the Zambezi River. Our team hadn't arrived yet by road, so instead of sitting miserably in the dirt we set up our sound system and ministered to the crowd that gathered around our strange flying machine. We started our service with lots of singing and dancing. Tom Jones and I preached. The Lord began to heal people, and we planted a church right then and there. The next morning we went back to minister to the new Christians. We asked the Holy Spirit to come to these men, women and children, and they were so easily filled. They have no resistance to the Gospel. We laid hands on them, and one by one they spoke in tongues. One of their men is going to our Bible school in Dondo and will pastor that group. We've never been in a time like this. We are seeing what our hearts have cried out for all these years.

Pastor José, our provincial pastor in Maputo, told us his mother had been praying for revival for many, many years. He remembers hearing her cry for revival since he was a tiny little boy. She told him that before she died all she wanted was to see revival in Mozambique, and her son married. When we married José and Linda one Sunday, his mother said, "Now I can go home to be with Jesus. I've seen the revival I've prayed for all these years, and I've seen my son married in the church." A week later she went to be with Jesus.

He's calling out radical servant-lovers. He's breathing His life into His sleeping Church. His lovers will carry His presence, and the hungry won't resist anymore.

Chapter 10

Postscript: Jars of Clay

But we have this treasure in jars of clay to show that this all-surpassing power is from God and not from us. We are hard pressed on every side, but not crushed; perplexed, but not in despair; persecuted, but not abandoned; struck down, but not destroyed. We always carry around in our body the death of Jesus, so that the life of Jesus may also be revealed in our body. For we who are alive are always being given over to death for Jesus' sake, so that his life may be revealed in our mortal body.

2 Corinthians 4:7–11

It would be easy to list our testimonies of victory and create the impression that we have come to live a life of protected ease, blessing and fruitfulness. But our life of faith is continually and increasingly put to the test, not only revealing our flaws, but also His mercies, which are new every morning. We die daily, and daily we are raised again after having lost all reliance on ourselves. We are only in the beginning stages of learning to trust God, who raises the dead.

We are very conscious that we are not in control of this revival movement, and that looking after so many churches is a project far over our heads. The plight of the poor and lost of the entire African continent weighs down on us and would crush us if Jesus did not intervene. But we don't want to be kept from knowing the world's problems. Neither do we want to be spared from undergoing His discipline and training, by which we will share in His holiness and be useful to Him, prepared for every good work.

So as jars of clay we enter the spiritual fray by faith, straining toward what is ahead. It is amazing to us that He is able to qualify us for this fight. Just when we think we know how to minister to the one, a thousand or ten thousand present themselves urgently and desperately. We barely find time and patience to handle one drastic crisis only to run into ten more the same day. We pour out love and compassion one minute only to run dry and turn irritable the next. We preach our hearts out and see vast response only to encounter great ignorance, misunderstanding and hardness of heart the next. We receive miracles of financial provision only to be robbed and cheated on a grand scale the next. We teach faith, but begging continues on all sides. We preach power, but the hungry die before us, forgotten by the wealthy. We preach unity in the Spirit, but we have to deal with jealousies and offenses of all kinds. Our marriage, family and closest friendships are under assault every day from intense stress and impossible demands.

We are asked for counsel and direction as though we have the answers at all times—How do we become missionaries? How will I support myself? Can I please have a truck? How can I run the churches in my district without a phone, an address or even a pencil and piece of paper? We haven't eaten in weeks. How will I get to Bible school? What will happen to my family? Can you pay for my child's funeral and buy a coffin for us?

Every day requests come pouring into the office for finances, always for good, legitimate, desperately needed things. Heidi faces long queues all day long, every person in a tragic, difficult situation needing help. We see their lined faces and cracked, weathered skin, survivors of Africa's harsh realities. There are so few employers to send them to, so few missions who will take them in, so few other churches that will teach them how to live the Christian life. Everyone is at capacity, stretched to the limit, unable to do more.

Yet in the face of everything Satan can do, we maintain that there is always enough. We were advised to give up and leave Mozambique years ago, but we are still here because we believe the Gospel of Jesus Christ is adequate, and that in Him we are more than conquerors even as we lay down as sheep to be slaughtered. We are, in fact, hard pressed, perplexed and struck down—but not destroyed. We don't know how we will endure through the day or the week. We don't know how to please everyone, answer all our e-mail, send all our reports, pay for every need and minister with anointing night and day. We don't know how to keep all our staff, brief all our visitors, reassure the disappointed, lift the weak and provide clear direction for everyone. We are only a few jars of clay! Yet Jesus has revealed that because He died, there is always enough, and we will never deny that revelation.

There are over 180,000 AIDS orphans in Mozambique, over 400,000 in Malawi and 1,000,000 in Kenya. Here in Mozambique the prime minister has admitted that this country is facing collapse because so many teachers, policemen and health workers are dying of AIDS. Millions in southern Africa are facing death in the near future from the especially deadly combination of AIDS and famine. Organized crime and drug traffic undermine the economic growth figures that are cited. We are surrounded by extreme crisis.

Yes, we are seeing a great revival and move of God, one that we have cried out for all our lives, and we are unspeakably grateful. But our appetite has just been whetted. We are only jars of clay, but God's power is made perfect in weakness. And in all our weakness we will keep submitting ourselves to Him, that we can see His glory, that we can be part of His answer for Africa and the world. If He can raise ten from the dead, He can raise a hundred or ten thousand. If He can double our chicken and bread in one meal, He can feed a whole village or province. If He can change my heart or yours, He can change anyone. We have seen too much, we have tasted too much of the powers of the age to come, we have drunk too deeply of the love of God to ever say again, "No, there isn't enough. That's all Jesus has. I'm sorry."

No, we will always say, "Go to Him. Eat and drink of Him. What we don't have, He has. Be desperate for Him. Have faith in Him. Love Him. Look into His eyes. His body and blood are enough for all who will receive Him." And we know we will see more revival. We will keep testifying to the Gospel of God's grace. We and the rest of the Body of Christ will persevere and do greater things than Jesus did on earth, because He is good and has prepared these things for us to do from before the foundation of the world.